A Pride of Kin

A WARDLAW BOOK

A Pride of Kin

by Callie Coe Wilson

and Ellen Walker Rienstra

TEXAS A&M UNIVERSITY PRESS

COLLEGE STATION

Library of Congress Cataloging in Publication Data

Wilson, Callie Coe, 1917–
A pride of kin.

"A Wardlaw book."
1. Hook family. 2. Hardin County (Tex.)—Bibliography.
3. Wilson, Callie Coe, 1917– . I. Rienstra, Ellen
Walker. II. Title.
F392.H37H589 1985 976.4'15704'0922 [B] 84-16341
ISBN 0-89096-226-X

Parts of this manuscript have appeared in a different form in *Tales from the Big Thicket*, edited by Francis E. Abernethy (Austin: University of Texas Press, 1966), and are used by permission.

Manufactured in the United States of America
First Edition

TO

William and Martha Hooks

AND

THEIR NUMEROUS PROGENY

Contents

Acknowledgments

It is impossible for us to thank all those friends and relatives, both living and dead, who, throughout their lives and ours, regaled us with so many of the stories we tell here. However, there are a few of the living to whom we can and must extend our thanks: to our kin, Esther Hooks Walker, Thomas A. Hooks, and Dr. Henry Allen Hooks, for their especially generous contributions to our cache of family legends, and to our friend, Miss Mary Montgomery, for her timely recollections of those choice stories told to her by our late Uncle Ben Hooks. We also owe thanks to those members of our family who ransacked their attics and family archives for material pertaining to our twice- or thrice-told tales: William Hooks Parker, Patsy Marshall Warnick, Lorene and Joe Coe, Thomas Sidney Hooks, Ruth Hooks Armour, Herring Coe, and Mariella and Hugh Isaac Taylor. To Nancy Wilson Scanlan we owe thanks for her fine photography, and to John H. Walker for his splendid rubbing from the gravestone of our great-grandparents.

We are deeply indebted to Dona Fertitta for the untiring hours she spent at the typewriter and the unabridged dictionary, preparing our manuscript; to Betty Cuthrell for the inspired introduction to our present publishers; and to George F. Scheer for his literary expertise and valuable time, unstintingly given us when we needed it the most.

—CCW and EWR

Publisher's Acknowledgment

The Texas A&M University Press is privileged to add its imprint to this Wardlaw Book. The designation claims a special place in the list of Texas A&M publications.

Supported with funds inspired by the initiative of Chester Kerr, former head of Yale University Press, this book, along with its companion volumes, perpetuates the association of Frank H. Wardlaw's name with a select group of titles appropriate to his reputation as man of letters, distinguished publisher, and founder of three university presses.

Donors of these funds represent a wide cross-section of Frank Wardlaw's admirers, including colleagues from scholarly presses throughout the country as well as those from other callings who recognize and applaud the many contributions that he has made to scholarship, literature, and publishing in his four decades of active service.

The Texas A&M University Press acknowledges with profound appreciation these donors.

Mr. Herbert S. Bailey, Jr.
Mr. Robert Barnes
Mr. W. Walker Cowan
Mr. John Ervin, Jr.
Mr. William D. Fitch
Mr. August Frugé
Mr. David H. Gilbert
Mr. Kenneth Johnson
Mr. Chester Kerr
Mr. Robert T. King
Mr. Carl C. Krueger, Jr.
Mr. John H. Kyle
Mrs. S. M. McAshan, Jr.
Mr. Kenneth E. Montague
Mr. Edward J. Mosher
Mrs. Florence Rosengren

Mr. Jack Schulman
Mr. C. B. Smith
Mr. Richard A. Smith
Mr. Stanley Sommers
Dr. Frank E. Vandiver
Ms. Maud E. Wilcox
Mr. John Williams

Their bounty has assured that Wardlaw Books will be a special source of instruction and entertainment to the reading public for many years to come.

A Pride of Kin

Our expeditions are but tours, and come round again
at evening to the old hearth-side from which we set out.
—Henry David Thoreau

Prologue

I am not a genealogist. I am not interested in tracing the lineage of my family or in writing a chronological account of their personal history. A straight line may very well be the shortest distance between two points, whatever they are, but in my opinion the turn of a phrase affords a more attractive approach to any subject. My father's mother's people, the Hookses of Hardin County, Texas, had a natural aptitude for words—they could turn a phrase every way but loose. Arden Hooks, my second cousin, was an inveterate storyteller, and one of Daddy's brothers, my Uncle Bryant Coe, could take the flimsiest skein of truth and thereby hang a tale. It is on such tales that I have always hung, if not my implicit faith, certainly a fanatical interest. From childhood, I have been fascinated with family folklore. And it has usually been tales about the Hookses that have fed my fancy—gorged it, in fact.

They have a staying quality, these Hookses, that I can only describe as haunting. They have inhabited my imagination all my life, inexplicable ghosts, to be exorcised only by that bit of magic that created them in the first place, the turn of a phrase.

My cousin Ellen Rienstra, twenty years my junior but the same generation of Hookses, recently confessed to me that she, too, felt possessed by these ancestral apparitions.

That was when I suggested that we write about them, we

two, put them into words and catch them in their own trap, the example they, themselves, had so adroitly set. Ellen accepted the proposal. Once we got started, we got carried away. There were lots of straws in the prevailing wind, so, like the first little pig, we worked with straw. Let who will blow our constructions down.

—C. C. W.

1

The Family Cemetery

In Hardin County in Southeast Texas the soil is red, and the trees that grow deep in the earth (they are mostly pine trees) grow tall in the sky. The wind makes a song in the treetops. To some it is a mournful sound, lonesome and yearning; to others it is music, pure and simple. To the Hookses, who settled the county, it is music. To the early generations (my Grandmother Coe was Amanda Hooks) it was the measure to which their lives moved. To their descendants it is a strongly reverberating chord. I still remember the first time I felt such reverberation; it was at a family funeral the year I was eight years old.

Hooks descendants are legion. It was frequently said that the Hookses not only settled Hardin County but populated it. Through the years they have scattered—colorful leaves off a deciduous tree—and despite a certain clannishness, which is legendary, they are not and never have been a family for visiting. A story goes that my great-grandfather, William "Pap" Hooks, once passed the house of his brother Jim, whom he hadn't seen for ten years, without going in. It seems that on his way there he'd met a cousin, a reliable man, who'd assured him that Jim and all his family were doing fine, which was all my great-grandfather had wanted to know in the first place.

Family reunions were always occasions, like Christmas or county fairs. Everyone came and brought a cake or a ham and all their children. Family funerals were solemn occasions, and the Hookses gathered for them as naturally as blood flowing from a fresh wound congeals. The family cemetery is in the Piney Woods, between Beaumont and Kountze.

The year I was eight I was allowed to attend a family funeral for the first time. I don't remember who had died—a great-uncle, I think—but my father, who usually left such things up to my mother, had suddenly decided that my younger sister and I were old enough to observe family rites. Our mother didn't believe in taking children to funerals—I was too sensitive, she said, and Pat, my little sister, was entirely too young. But that time our father prevailed—there would be people at the cemetery who had never even seen his two youngest children, he pointed out. Mama was not impressed. We were living in Beaumont at the time, awfully close to Hardin County as the crow flies, but then, as most folks knew, the Hookses had never been ones to imitate the habits of another species. Pat and I went to the funeral—in a blue Chevrolet that belonged to our Uncle Wallace, Daddy's baby brother—and I was fascinated by the number of cars in the long procession.

"Are all those people really our cousins?" I asked Daddy.

"Aunts and uncles and cousins," he explained, "and a few old family friends—all come to pay their last respects."

The lengthy cortege that wound through the East Texas woods that day was the thread of an old story, a thread that I picked up and have been unwinding in my own imagination ever since. Its implications were my earliest intimations of continuity. Riding in that raveling string of cars, I felt for the first time in my life the strong pull of family ties. I am still irresistibly drawn by even the most distant connections to common ground.

The Hooks Cemetery is no more than a mile off the main highway, but that Sunday (the services were set for Sunday so that everyone could come) it seemed to me to be at the end of the world. A private road led to the cemetery gates, running like an unpruned vine through a stand of pines, twisting and turning as though it were alive. It was full of chuckholes and very narrow, hardly more than a converted cowpath. The cemetery grounds had at one time been a farm that belonged to our great-grandparents, Daddy said.

Time dragged, but at last the procession of cars pulled slowly into a clearing, and the drivers, keeping a careful lookout for stumps, parked at precarious angles. Car doors flew open, and a stream of people poured like spilled milk over the ground. Clutching at Daddy's hand, I felt my feet sinking into the soft leaf-mold floor of the clearing. Looking down, I saw the imprint of a cow's or a horse's hoof. Had it been the footprint of Pan, I couldn't have felt more transported. The cemetery itself was straight ahead.

I remember the sudden smell of freshly turned earth and cut flowers. I remember the sound of the wind in the trees, a sighing sound. I remember the feel of my hand in my father's hand. But most of all I remember all those Hookses. Men—in whose faces I searched for a resemblance to my father's, sometimes finding it—shook hands solemnly or quietly gripped each other's shoulders. Women kissed each other on slightly turned cheeks. Some of them kissed my father and Pat and me. There were lots of children—all cousins, I supposed—and some of them were even younger than Pat. Everyone spoke in lowered voices and all at the same time. There was a feeling of sad festivity.

"You and Pat stay close to me," Daddy said, releasing our hands, "or go find Joyce." Our older sister Joyce had come to the funeral in a separate car. She was in her twenties and had been coming to funerals at the Hooks Cemetery for a long time.

"Well, I'll declare," someone said, reaching out for Daddy's arm, "if it isn't Cousin Burrell. How are you, Burrell?"

He turned and embraced a pretty woman in a purple hat. "Good Lord," he exclaimed, "it's been a coon's age."

"Yes, isn't it awful the way we only get home for funerals," the woman said.

Daddy slipped his arm through hers and they talked together, turning up old memories as casually as if they were last year's canna bulbs. In all the conversations I overheard that day the buried past seemed to come up perennially.

"And these are our two little girls," Daddy said finally, presenting Pat and me. "This is Callie Mae, named for Callie, of course, and Ida's mother, and this is Pat. She isn't named for anyone, but, tell me, who do you think she looks like?"

The pretty cousin put her hand on Pat's head, as if she were bestowing her blessing. "Why, Burrell," she said, "she's the image of your mother."

"Isn't she," Daddy agreed. He had always thought so.

We all walked across the clearing together, like an exaltation of larks or a gaggle of geese. The grass was high, and I remember getting grass seed, as tenacious as ticks, on my ankles. I remember that I wanted to scratch but that Joyce had said we mustn't.

"It isn't ladylike," she'd explained.

The cemetery was in a grove of trees—not all pines. There were gums, oaks, magnolias, an old walnut tree, and sycamores hung with balls that looked like burnt-out Christmas tree lights.

"There it is, the Hooks Cemetery," Daddy said, and I remember the catch in his voice. It sounded like a lock that didn't work when you turned the key. "That's where all your Coe and Hooks kin are buried—your great-grandparents and your oldest sister who died when she was a baby, before any of the rest of you were born."

"Bernice," Pat said softly. "That's who it was, Bernice."

I don't remember what I had expected; surely my unbridled imagination had run away with me. My childhood had been enchanted by tales of my Hardin County kin, and the last resting place of so many of them was certainly hallowed ground as far as I was concerned. I do remember that I was not disappointed. I openly stared, another thing that Joyce had said we mustn't do.

The whole scene was like a fresh illustration in a familiar book. Moss hung like beards on the ancient trees, giving them the look of a venerable ancestry. Tombstones seemed to spring out of the ground like toadstools. Some of them had toppled over. The black iron fence around the family graveyard (outsiders buried outside the fence, Daddy said) resembled the simple line drawing of a child, something I might have done in the first grade, I remember thinking. An old pitcher pump, dripping water, stood at the gate, looking for all it was worth like a derelict mourner. I don't know why, but that old pump became a symbol to me, an emotional landmark.

The crowd moved slowly through the gate, as if, indeed, their last respects were the price of admission. In passing, the pretty cousin in the purple hat smiled at me. In perfect complicity, I smiled back. The solemnity of the occasion was not broken; it was sealed, like a private letter.

Everyone gathered around the new grave—red and raw, it looked to me like an open wound. The graves around it looked like scars, some of them only recently healed. The coffin was covered with a blanket of red roses, and over to one side, stacked carelessly on the ground, was a mound of flowers, sheaves of bronze chrysanthemums tied with taffeta ribbon and sprays of pink carnations and calla lilies. They had already begun to wilt.

I stood with Daddy and Pat and Joyce under a sweet-gum tree. Daddy got sweet-gum on his good suit, I remember. I couldn't follow the funeral service so my attention strayed.

Looking around, I saw a man behind another tree putting on his coat and changing his shoes. I knew immediately, although I had never seen him before, that he was my great-uncle Ben Hooks, a living legend in the family folklore that so fascinated me. It was said that he kept a fiddler at his large country home in Kountze, the way some people kept a gardener or a cow. It was also said that he personally supervised all the grave digging in the Hooks Cemetery, handling the shovel himself if the deceased happened to be a close relative.

"Howdy, Burrell," he said, walking up beside us. "We're burying one of the best today—and before his time too." I noticed that he had red clay under his fingernails.

"Ashes to ashes, dust to dust," the preacher said portentiously.

"He gave me my first shotgun, Ben," Daddy said.

I was enthralled by the number of tombstones, as I had been by the number of cars and the number of cousins in the clearing. I started counting them but stopped when I reached a hundred and started thinking about the people whose graves they marked. Daddy had told me a lot about them, pleased that I was interested in the old stories. None of the other children—there were five of us—seemed to care about them, except Joyce, who acted as if she had known them all along.

The first Hookses, Daddy said, had come from Georgia to Texas in the early days of its statehood. The cemetery was part of the first Hooks settlement in Hardin County, the original farm owned by William and Martha Hooks, our great-grandparents. They hadn't stayed there long, Daddy explained—they had moved on to another farm nearer Kountze, but they had always returned to bury their dead in the first Texas soil they had tilled. To their descendants these rites had become a family tradition, the grounds a family cemetery. The ancestral pride of the Hookses, famous throughout the area, was as geographical as it was genealogical. As William Faulkner called it, "the old haughty ancestral pride based not on any value but on an accident of geography." Some of those early Texas Hookses were as sure that they were made out of East Texas clay as they were that they were made in God's image—surer, as a matter of fact. The words "dust thou art, to dust returneth" meant to them the same dust in both cases. That's why I couldn't finish counting all the tombstones.

"He has gone to join his ancestors," the preacher said, and I envisioned another family reunion in heaven.

The circle that had formed around the grave finally broke, becoming once more a loosened chain of circumstances in which I was instantly entangled.

"How is Ida, Burrell?" someone asked.

"She's just fine," I volunteered. "She didn't want Pat and me to come. She thinks we're too young to go to funerals."

Joyce glared at me, and I knew that I had said something wrong.

"Kye," I felt Pat tugging at my sleeve, struggling for my attention.

"What is it?" I asked, relieved to get away.

"I found our name," she confided.

She led me to a large headstone of Texas granite and, leaning over as far as she could, pointed to the inscription. "See," she said proudly and spelled it out. "C-O-E. That's our name."

"Sure it is," I agreed. "This is our family cemetery. Everyone in here is kin to us, no matter what their name is. That's our grandmother's tombstone," I said.

"The one you're named for or the one I look like?" she wanted to know.

"The one you look like," I told her. "She had eyes as blue as cornflowers and twelve children. Daddy was the oldest and her favorite."

"How do you know?" Pat asked. "She didn't tell you."

"No one has to tell you some things," I said, inadvertently making an observation that since then has become a point of view.

"Are my eyes as blue as cornflowers?" Pat wondered.

"Not quite," I said. "They're diluted a little—by Mama's blood, I suppose."

"Isn't Mama's blood blue?" she asked anxiously.

"Sure," I said, "bluer than anybody's. But her eyes are brown—like mine."

We had spit on our fingers and were cleaning out the letters cut in our grandmother's stone when Joyce discovered us.

"What in the world are you doing?" she demanded. "Papa wants you. He wants to show you off, so stand up straight and speak when you're spoken to. Not before," she added, looking hard at me.

"That's Bernice's grave," I said, pointing to it. "Uncle Wallace showed it to me. If she had lived, she'd be older than you."

"Here they are," Daddy announced as Joyce dutifully delivered us into his outstretched hands.

We became the center of a small crowd, much to my delighted consternation. Everyone made over us, as if we were celebrities or had just escaped some awful danger, like drowning in the creek or being kidnapped by gypsies.

"Would you have known them anywhere else?" Daddy asked the group of relatives who were beaming on us.

"Anywhere in the world," some woman insisted.

"They're Coes all right," everyone agreed.

The circle expanded. A young woman carrying a baby on her hip appeared on the periphery. She was followed by several small children, one of them clinging to her skirt. I stared again, in spite of all of Joyce's admonitions. I had never seen so many children who looked so much alike. They were all about the same size, and they all had hair the color of straw. They were all barefooted. One of the little boys had sat in the dirt, and the seat of his pants was red; anyone could see that he was soaking wet. The baby's nose was running, so I offered his mother my handkerchief.

"You can keep it if you don't have one," I told her.

"Callie Mae!" Joyce said sharply.

"I was only trying to be helpful," I explained later. "They're our cousins, aren't they?"

Several young women exchanged glances. "Creek-bottom cousins," one of them murmured under her breath, but I heard her.

"They're fixing to fill in the grave," someone called, and I remember seeing Uncle Ben Hooks pick up a shovel and throw in the first scoop of dirt.

After the grave filling, everyone seemed to drift away in different directions—some in search of a headstone that was hidden by the long grass or covered with yellow jasmine; some to show a small boy the grave of his great-great-grandfather; and some just to start pulling up the weeds that had almost taken over the place since the last family funeral. The preacher had left in his model-T Ford, and the immediate family had been taken home in a Cadillac that belonged to one of the rich relatives. Those who remained, according to custom, were clearing up the litter and the questions of family lineage that seemed to keep coming up. A gregarious group had gathered around a large block of marble that looked to me like an ancient monolith—it was black with age—but was actually the double tombstone of William and Martha Hooks, our great-grandparents, Joyce told me. The two-grave plot had a marble curb all around it, and in the center there was a marble urn filled with wild honeysuckle. Seemingly set off to itself, the enclosed space had the aura of a designated shrine, I thought.

Two girls with their arms full of magnolia leaves suddenly appeared from out of the woods. "We're hunting Cousin Jo's grave," one of them said. "We want to put these leaves on it. Remember how she loved magnolia leaves?"

"Come on and help us hunt," the other girl invited Joyce. Pat and I tagged along.

"Cousin Jo is over there with the Chances," a voice called after us. "She was double kin, remember."

When we found her grave, there was a bunch of shattered pink roses in a wide-mouthed fruit jar on it. The water in the jar was green and slimy.

"Here, go empty this," Joyce said, handing me the jar. "But for heaven's sake be careful and don't get that slimy stuff on your dress. It's awful. Pat, you can help pull up weeds," she added.

I felt important, although I did hate being bossed, and I struck off by myself in search of a trash can. I remember wandering alone among the family graves, feeling like a spirit, disembodied but abiding, two words I had picked up from the preacher's sermon. I wasn't afraid, although I was usually scared of my shadow. The names on the tombstones were familiar names—Coe, Hooks, Chance, Roberts, and Turner—names that had played active parts in Daddy's stories. There were flowers on a lot of the graves, brightly colored zinnias, cape jasmine, seven-sister roses. Most of the flowers were in fruit jars. Some of the jars were broken. On one grave there was a single red canna in a coke bottle.

I couldn't find a trash can, I remember, so I walked over to the edge of the woods to throw the dead roses away. Intent on my errand, I almost stumbled over a little girl about my own age who, with her pants pulled down, was squatting behind a pine tree. I was flabbergasted.

"Well, if that isn't about the worst thing I ever saw," I said, "even if you are a cousin. You ought to be ashamed of yourself."

The girl stared up at me, unmoved. "Why?" she asked innocently. "My mama doesn't care if I pee-pee on Sunday."

I was speechless. I turned on my heel and started back the way I had come, to rejoin Pat and Joyce or to look for Daddy. Suddenly, I recovered my power of speech. "Creek-bottom cousin," I murmured under my breath.

I was stopped by a group of people who were taking flowers off the new grave.

"We're going to divide up these pot plants," one of them said. "There must be a hundred, and you all know how he was about sharing, especially with his own family. Come help," she said to me and handed me two pots of red geraniums.

I put the geraniums on the graves of my grandparents, Henry Isaac and Amanda Hooks Coe. I put a yellow chrysanthemum plant on Bernice's grave. Mama loved yellow chrysanthemums.

"Thanks," the woman who had asked me to help said when we were through. "You did a lot. You're a Coe, aren't you?"

"Yes," I said. "I'm Callie Mae Coe, Burrell Coe's daughter, Amanda Coe's granddaughter, the great-granddaughter of William and Martha Hooks." The words fell like perfectly selected pieces into place, forming an integral part of an expansive pattern, a mosaic. I remember saying them over and over, to a deaf old man who nodded, to a lady who stooped to kiss my cheek.

"Good lord, child," someone finally said. "We know who you are."

That was when I first felt the reverberations of the past in my bloodstream, like the distant beating of a tribal drum. Carefully picking my way among the tombstones so as not to step on any of the graves—Joyce had said not to—I went to meet my father and my sisters. I was triumphant. I had red clay on my Sunday shoes, and the wind was singing in the pine trees.

On the way home, Pat leaned over the back of the car seat and nudged our father.

"Daddy," she asked him, "who died?"

His answer was philosophical. He said, "Hush, Pat."

—C. C. W.

2

The Family Homestead

I suppose most people—even the sanest—are haunted by something. We all seem to have our own personal ghosts. Perhaps I have even more than most of us, which is understandable, considering my background. My mother was a Hooks of Hardin County, and the Hooks family, with their natural propensity for storytelling, used even the most formidable of family ghosts for their own private purposes—the instruction and entertainment of their progeny. The children of this family were regaled with the exploits of their ancestors the way most children were read bedtime stories or told fairy tales. As a consequence, they were as familiar with the personalities of their departed relatives as they were with those of Tom Thumb or Alice in Wonderland. I, like my cousin Callie Wilson, was one of those children. No wonder we're both haunted.

The setting for my own ghostly fantasies is, commonly enough, an old house. This one-story white frame house, built in the waning years of the nineteenth century, still stands right outside of Kountze, tucked comfortably away on a knoll in the East Texas Piney Woods, just off the Saratoga Road. An unprepossessing structure, it was built in the shape of a simple square, its high-peaked roof making it look more vertical than a typical East Texas dogtrot house. Nevertheless, it appears to my imagination as a prototype of all in East Texas that is traditional and as a stronghold of my own East Texas inheritance. I can't remember when it was not an integral part of my memory.

Henry Allen Hooks, called "Bud" by everyone who knew him, was my maternal grandfather and the man who built this house. He built it for his mother, right after his father's death, on a spot that his father had chosen. After William and Martha Hooks moved away from their last farm and into town, they still found innumerable excuses for getting back into the country—to visit their daughter Lucina, who had married and moved to Old Hardin, to pick up feed for their livestock or just to have a look around. During their frequent forays down the old Saratoga Road, Pap, with his enduring eye for a good piece of land, had fallen in love with the wooded knoll just to the west of Kountze. Every time they drove past it, he would say to Ma that someday he intended to buy that land and build a house on it.

He died before he realized his dream. After his death, Ma bought the land, and Bud, their youngest child, built the house according to her specifications. Bud lived with Ma until she died, barely three years after Pap's death, then continued living in the house himself until his own death nearly a half-century later. He died some years before I was born, yet during my childhood his spirit, kept alive for me by stories told to me by my family, still presided over the homestead. According to the inscription on his tombstone, he is buried in the Hooks Cemetery with all the rest of the Hookses, but, for me, his presence has always remained in his house.

When I was a little girl in Beaumont, we often went back to Hardin County, mainly to visit my grandmother, who still lived in the old family homestead, but partly to revisit the old house itself. My brother and sister and I always looked forward to these periodic visits, and by the time we set out for Kountze in our old Ford station wagon, our imaginations—mine, anyway—were running away with us. As we crossed Pine Island Bayou into Hardin County, plunging deeper and deeper into the piney woods, time, for me, always slowed, stopped, then began almost imperceptibly to move backward.

Our pilgrimage—because that's what it was—always ended in the big front yard of the family homestead. The yard was full of enormous trees: oaks, sycamores, and magnolias. Oddly enough, there were no pines on the place—they had long since, for whatever reason, been relegated to the woods that completely surrounded the property. If our visit occurred in the summer—and it usually did—I always looked hastily around to see if there were any blue hydrangeas blooming. Hydrangeas were naturally pink, my grandmother had told me; their blooms were blue only when there was metal in the soil. My grandfather had planted tin cans in the holes with some of their bushes, she had said, and I was always eager to see if their metallic magic was still working. It usually was.

An old-fashioned iron fence went all the way around the yard, carefully enclosing it. When we opened the front gate, the handle made a clinking sound against the gatepost, as if to announce our approach. Two huge old camellia trees, pink perfections I believe, stood like stocky sentinels on either side of the gate, and we stepped in between these trees onto a brick-and-earth walk mossy with age and moisture. Its pungent odor always tickled my nostrils and titillated my imagination. At the twisted roots of the giant oak trees, green moss grew profusely in rain-sculpted patterns, forming tiny cliffs, canyons, and forests that further excited my fancy.

As we eagerly made our way up the walk, a familiar figure invariably materialized in the darkness of the deeply recessed porch—my grandmother, Esther Hooks, the gracious chatelaine of this backwoods domain. She was a small, fine-boned woman with a straight back and a subtle air of quiet omnipotence. She always wore a dark cotton dress, a small gold bar pin fastened neatly under its high collar, and black lace-up shoes of the kind that I privately thought of as "old ladies' shoes." I never saw her dressed any other way. She quietly but warmly made us welcome.

The interior of the house also had a special odor—a cedar-chest smell of things old and dear. The entrance hall was always dimly lit. Looking high up toward the ceiling, I could just barely discern my grandfather's collection of animal heads, their eyes staring glassily into space. There were heads of an enormous elk, several deer, an antelope, and one old goat with gnarled horns. He was mounted over the entrance to the back porch. There had been a moose head at one time, someone said, but the moths had eaten it, and it had been banished to the attic. I remember seeing it there years later, looming dimly between an old chest and a huge stack of magazines. It smelled like mothballs.

In one wing of the house, there was an impeccable little sitting room with a glassed-in bookcase that held my grandfather's—and what was left of my great-grandfather's—library. It included complete sets of Shakespeare, Dickens, Cooper, and Scott, several volumes of Edgar Allan Poe, and an old dog-eared copy of *The Travels of Baron Munchausen*, those rollicking adventures of the world's greatest liar. My mother told me that it had been Pap's favorite book. Once when I was browsing through it, a scrap of yellowed newspaper fell out—Pap's improvised bookmark, no doubt.

In the other wing of the house, there was a bedroom and another fireplace whose mantle held a fascinating assortment of objects: a metal horse that looked like a Remington statue, attesting to the family's love of fine horses, two plaster hunting dogs that my grandfather had bought at a Texas health spa, and an old green whiskey bottle full of homemade camphor, standing ready for medical emergencies. I used to beg to be allowed to pull the stopper out of that bottle, just to sniff its strong aroma.

The room was dominated by an enormous old four-poster bed, made of black walnut in Tyler County by my grandmother's family. It stood so high off the floor I had to be lifted up onto it. A crack ran all the way across its massive headboard—a casualty of its trip to Hardin County, I was told. I remember tracing that crack with my finger. I would often lie with my head on the bolster and, looking up, would examine all the pictures on the walls around the room. They were all portraits of the Hooks family. Their faces looked down at me from old-fashioned gilt frames. Like the heads of the animals, they stared impassively from their positions at a continually changing world.

To me, the Hookses in these pictures lived—they were old friends as well as relatives. Many nights, when the old Seth Thomas wall clock in the fireplace bedroom struck the hour, those pictures would come alive. As my grandmother softly sang a familiar lullaby, the old house would become peopled with a host of friendly shades.

"There's Pap, my great-grandfather," I would recite to myself, thinking that he looked like God, "and there's Ma with her glasses on top of her head. There's Uncle Lum, with his red hair and freckles; he was a mathematical genius and died young. There's Uncle Day, the wild one, and Uncle Buck, who was a ladies' man. And there's my Granddaddy, the handsomest of them all."

It was invariably the ghost of my grandfather who loomed the largest. His personality permeated the whole house. This was not entirely accidental. His hat remained where he had hung it, on the old hall tree just inside the front door, along with a collection of his hunting horns. The hat was size 7⅞, I remember.

Many of his other possessions were also right where he had left them. His desk still stood in the fireplace bedroom. Inside it, there was a rock-hard, partially bitten plug of his chewing tobacco and a blown-out ostrich egg he had once tried—and failed—to make hatch. His gun cabinet, with his firearms still in it, stood next to his desk. His clothes were still in the dresser drawers. He was continuously present in daily conversation. It was almost as if the active life of the house had ceased with his death and had settled, thereafter, into a gentle twilight of remembrance and regret, content with the presence of familial ghosts.

It was Arden Hooks, Bud's son, my mother's brother and my beloved uncle, who, during the years of my impressionable youth, was the medium through which most of those friendly Hooks spectres made their regular incursions into my imagination. Arden brought them to life through the stories he told me, and in my childish mind, he himself, their emissary, embodied all those magical qualities possessed by the people he talked about. To me, he was the quintessential Hooks.

He figured largely in my memories of those early childhood visits to the old Hooks homestead, a natural—if not slightly supernatural—personage who always appeared when he was least expected. Halfway through an early breakfast in the kitchen, my siblings and I would glance out the back door to see him moving silently up the walk; in the middle of our evening games, he would suddenly materialize at the front gate. When we began to venture into the woods surrounding the old homestead, we would sometimes encounter him there, enjoying a solitary walk.

I often joined him on his walks, especially on those around the yard, eager to hear the stories he would tell. It was just as if I hadn't heard them a hundred times over. It was the way he told them that kept me fascinated. He was one of the true tellers of tales, this family folklorist.

"See those two big pecan trees over there," he would say. "The ones near the house? Dad planted them at Ma's instruction. She had to have nut trees wherever she lived—thought they kept the lightning from striking the house."

I would grin, encouraging him to go on.

"This yard used to be full of outbuildings," he'd explain, "all of them built by Dad. His inventiveness really had Jeffersonian implications. He built an outdoor bathroom that was three stories high. It had a gasoline engine in it that pumped water all the way up to the third floor. The ground floor had a big bathtub in it. The toilet was in a separate building, farther away from the house," he'd add. "Neither Dad nor Uncle Ben liked the idea of having a toilet inside, much to Mother's and Aunt Zula's chagrin."

Sure enough, the old family homestead did not have an indoor bathroom until several years after my grandfather died, I recall.

"The most unusual of Dad's constructions was a storm cellar," my woodsy Virgil would continue. "Of course, there never have been many cyclones in our part of Texas, but a spell of freak weather once spawned a few in Batson Prairie, and everybody in Kountze started building cellars like they were cow barns. Dad's was surely the most original—a brick platform built ten or twelve feet deep into the family water well."

I can still hear his amused chuckle, and see his usually somber eyes assume a sustained twinkle, like stars reflected in still water; he enjoyed his old stories as much as I did.

His father had at one time kept the yard full of cages and pens filled with every kind of bird and animal imaginable, he said. It had evidently been a sort of zoo. According to Arden's story, the Kountze people used to walk up on Sunday afternoons to show it off to visitors or just to see for themselves the latest addition to Bud Hooks's menagerie. This menagerie included rabbits, raccoons, ring-necked pheasants, squirrels, half-wild turkeys, numerous deer, peacocks, and a cage full of doves for my Aunt Allie. No doubt there would have been ostriches too if that ill-fated ostrich egg had hatched.

Although this hobby of my grandfather's gave much pleasure to his friends and neighbors, I have heard that he was later accused of being indirectly responsible for the East Texas plague of armadillos. Some friends had once brought him a pair from South America, knowing his fondness for exotic animals. He had penned them up in his yard, but, as was their wont, they had dug a tunnel under the fence and escaped. There was no further sign of them until their offspring began to appear in the East Texas woods.

The legendary hunter Ben Lilly once gave him two Mexican lion cubs, Arden said. He kept them for awhile, then traded them to the Houston Zoo for an elk—why, I suppose only he knew. He kept the elk until it became dangerous, then gave it back to the zoo. Arden said they heard later that it killed its keeper.

"Dad got his love of animals from Pap, I guess," he mused. "He got a lot of things from Pap, but then we all did. The Hookses are a breed apart. I can recognize one a mile away."

They were certainly recognizable ghosts, I conceded.

I remember one time, however, when a real flesh-and-blood Hooks appeared to me as his own ghost. It was my great-uncle Ben Hooks, the leading figure in many of the family stories I'd enjoyed, and it was on one particular visit back to the family homestead.

"Before the week is over, I'll take you over to see your Uncle Ben," Mama had promised us. I could hardly contain my excitement throughout the week.

Late that Saturday afternoon, we all—my mother, my grandmother, my sister and brother and I—paid the proposed call on Uncle Ben. We set out in a comfortable group down a back lane, *the* lane, we'd always called it. I remember that the odor of wild honeysuckle on the fence hung heavy in the cooling air, and that my bare feet sent up little pink puffs of dust from the red dirt road.

Uncle Ben's house, just down the road, was a large Victorian structure with a big front porch that extended across its front and all around one side. We were greeted at the front steps by Aunt Zula, Uncle Ben's wife. She welcomed us onto the porch, where, engulfed in an enormous rocking chair, the legendary Ben Hooks sat quietly in the cool of the evening, an old man marking his remaining time.

"Hello, Ben," my grandmother said.

"Miss Essie," Uncle Ben courteously acknowledged his brother's widow.

"Uncle Ben, it's Esther," my mother spoke up loudly. Uncle Ben was hard of hearing. "I've brought my children to see you. This is Esther Ellen, this is Homer, and this is Judy."

"Hello, Esther," Uncle Ben said to her in a thin, dry voice that seemed to me to crackle with unwanted age. Could a legend really fade, I wondered? Could a man really become his own ghost? Then, raising his head, Uncle Ben fixed on us a sharp blue stare that defied any such spectral thoughts. I felt reassured.

"Mighty fine children you've got there," he said. Mama looked proud while we grinned with embarrassed pleasure. For a few moments Uncle Ben made quietly reminiscent conversation with my mother and grandmother. I only overheard fragments of their talk, which I pieced together in a patchwork pattern all my own. Too soon we turned to go; Uncle Ben tired very easily these days, my grandmother had warned us. As he told us goodbye, his eyes suddenly filled with an old man's easy tears. "Bud's grandchildren," he murmured sadly, "and he never lived to know them."

I revisited the old Hooks homestead in Kountze recently. It is still in the family, owned by one of Allie's sons, William Hooks Parker, nicknamed "Buddy" for his grandfather. At the time of my visit, the summer afternoon was nearly gone, dissolving imperceptibly into the velvet evening, and I could see at the edge of the woods the first green-and-gold pinpoints of the lightning bugs. The old house dreamed under the ancient trees, about to be enveloped in the soft Thicket night. The gate clinked as I stepped through it onto the walk. A slight breeze touched my face, bringing with it the scent of honeysuckle from the woods. The trees in the yard were half in shadow from the onset of the summer dusk, and as I glanced toward them I seemed to hear the sound of children's voices, tired and comfortable, anticipating the call to supper, but unwilling to quit their monotonous counting game:

> William Trembletoe, he's a good fisherman;
> Catches hens, puts 'em in pens.
> Wire, briar, limber lock;
> Sit and sing 'til twelve o'clock.
> O-U-T spells out go you,
> You old dirty dishrag, you.

One of those voices was my own.

—E. W. R.

3

William Hooks, Pioneer

Folktales, especially family folktales, are traditions that are none too carefully handed down from one generation to another. They can be outrageous exaggerations or simple understatements. They can be dreams that never quite came true or stark realities redressed for a better showing. They can be—and are in the Hooks family—a private literature.

Of course, in these accrued annals there are many conflicting stories; there are even alternate versions of the family's origin. One group of genealogists claim we are of English descent, the line having been traced back to the family of Robert Hooke, the famous seventeenth-century physicist; a second group contends that, although the Hookses did live in England for over three hundred years, they are originally from Ireland, the name deriving from the fact that they lived on a "hook" of land extending into Waterford Harbor. No one seems to know—or care—when they dropped the *e* or added the *s* to the name. It was possibly after there got to be so many of them.

I have no idea when the first Hooks came to America—I am reasonably sure, however, that he was followed closely by other members of his family. They are an aggregate breed. When you've seen one Hooks, you may not have seen them all, but chances are that sooner or later you will.

At any rate, whatever the prior facts, in 1833, my great-

great-grandfather, George Hooks, a North Carolina planter, moved to Georgia, and it was from there that his progeny (and my immediate antecedents) began their trek to Texas. It was the last major migration of the flock. The tales, however, go on.

The central character in these tales is William Hooks, affectionately known in both family circles and the surrounding area as "Pap." To many of his descendants, he was their prime progenitor, as original as Adam, as blessed as Abraham. He was my great-grandfather.

William and his wife, Martha Collier Hooks, came from Early County, Georgia, to Southeast Texas in 1848, a date almost everyone in the family is agreed upon. They came in a covered wagon drawn by oxen, part of a family caravan formed by William and three of his brothers—George, Allen, and Austin Hooks. Allen's wife was my great-grandmother's sister. Double first and second cousins abound in the Hooks family—they have always believed in closed alliances. There are several stories, of course, as to why the Hooks brothers left Georgia. One is that they were simply caught up in the popular urge to move westward. Another is that the Collier girls, my great-grandmother and her sister, were fleeing the machinations of an evil stepmother. I have always favored the second story. The Hookses I know (and have heard about) have seldom been moved by other people's urges, and no folklore is quite complete without a tale about a wicked stepmother. Whatever its urgency, that caravan was the harbinger of my East Texas heritage.

There are several stories about the trip, none of them authenticated, of course, since there are no written records. The Hookses were never ones for keeping diaries or journals, it seems, relying, as they always did, on their recollections and their reputations as raconteurs. The trek, I've been told, was a painfully slow one, taking almost two months, the clumsy wagons crawling along the roads and across the meadows at a snail's pace, bearing, like the snail, the top-heavy burden of their own abodes. They were crammed with a household's paraphernalia—bedsteads and huge slabs of bacon, the family Bible, and an assortment of pots and pans. The women rode with children on their laps, the men with shotguns across their knees. The countryside, still untamed, was rife with lurking dangers. It was necessary for them to keep a constant lookout for Indians, as well as for white renegades who were apt to rob their more prosperous fellow travelers.

In one of the wagons there was a hide-bottom rocking chair. On warm nights, after camp had been made, someone said, the sisters-in-law took turns rocking their babies to sleep. Homesickness and expectation surely vied in their hearts as, softly crooning the old Georgia camp songs, they watched their older children eagerly adjusting to the constantly changing scene, stretching their short legs to explore new ground, providently collecting fireflies in empty fruit jars to light their way. At the time, my great-grandparents had four children: Lum, who was nine; Day, who was six; Lucina, called "Cine," the only girl, who was four; and Buck, the baby, who was just a year old.

My great-grandfather was the leader of the expedition—apparently he was a man who took initiative as naturally as he took his time. I was told that on Sundays he read aloud from the family Bible and addressed himself personally to the Lord. Of course, with no calendar, he couldn't tell Sunday from any other day, so, according to the story, he would simply pick a day when he thought the caravan might need special guidance and designate it as the Sabbath—to be kept holy. A conceivable margin of error provided him with practical leeway; I understand he sometimes needed it. Once, they say, when his voice was raised in conversational supplication, his son Lum tugged frantically at his coattail and begged for his permission to go rabbit hunting. It seems that Lum, his eyes reverently lowered while his father prayed, had just seen three plump rabbits escaping into the underbrush. Parental permission for the hunt was granted, and that night, over a huge pot of rabbit stew, William Hooks confessed that he had quite possibly miscalculated. That week, he said, Sunday would not roll around until the following day—at which time, he assured everyone, he would thank God for His succulent provision. Evidently, game was harder to get than the ear of the Lord, at least out in open country.

On his trek to Texas, young Lum shot his first deer, providing his family with a venison feast, but before they actually arrived at their destination in Hardin County, the Hookses, I am sure, had had their first taste of both coon and possum. I am equally sure that it was not their last.

Finding water seems to have been their principal concern, however, especially since my great-grandmother, reputedly as firm as she was fastidious, insisted upon keeping her wagon and everything in it spotlessly clean. What with godliness on the one hand and cleanliness right next to it, I'm surprised the caravan arrived in Texas as soon as it did.

There must have been many incidents, both fortuitous and near fatal, along the way; certainly the most unusual one involved my great-grandfather's brother, Austin Hooks. The story goes that, while driving his oxcart across a river, Austin, an impetuous pioneer, accidentally drowned one of his oxen. A perfectionist, he became so furious with his unbalanced team (as well as with the unbalanced scales of justice) that he deliberately killed his other ox, burned his wagon, and walked back to Georgia, starting out again, more calmly (and with a third ox tied to his tailgate) the following year. After finally arriving safely, he is said to have settled down—somewhat, I suppose—in Southeast Texas for the rest of his life, a strange man even in an unconventional clan like the Hookses. Some of his offspring were also rather idiosyncratic. Gus Hooks, the most colorful character and convenient scapegoat in Hooks folklore, was his son.

When they first reached Texas, the Hooks contingent, shy only of Austin, settled in Tyler County. Some of them are still there, but William Hooks, for one, stayed only briefly. By the end of 1850, he was farming in Hardin County; he had set a house down in a clump of pines and planted cotton and sugar cane in the palmetto swamps and briar patches. He had staked a claim that was later to become a boast, at least among his descendants. He was a provident man; out of the red clay of Hardin County, "the sorriest farming land in the state," some folks said, he fed a rapidly growing family and a robust ambition. That East Texas red clay is still feeding the imaginations of some of his progeny.

Instinctively innovative, he was the first man in his part of Texas to fence in his farm, building the split-log fence himself, with the help of his older boys, not only to keep the predatory animals out of his crops but to satisfy his wife's sense of security. With his brother-in-law James Collier, who came to Texas a few years later, he formed a productive partnership. Together, they constructed their own cotton gin, they themselves carving out some of the pieces with their pocket knives. They also built a water mill big enough to furnish power for both grinding corn and cutting lumber. Although the first Hooks family lumber company was in Hooks Switch and owned by three of William's sons, its precocious forerunner was successfully performing years earlier on the Hooks farm just slightly south of Kountze. William Hooks was the independent operator.

He was a true pioneer; he was also a real eccentric, establishing some outrageous prerogatives that were later incorporated into family legend. People said that he plowed his fields in his shirttail; he disliked the constrictions of conventional dress, and he refused to be encumbered by custom. Furthermore, they said, he sat on his porch at the close of day just as casually clad, his chair tilted at a comfortable angle, his feet propped up on the bannisters, a small negro boy stationed at the front gate to signal if a female approached.

He had an understanding wife. While he struggled with the land, exulting in his slightest toe hold, she fended with impending nature for their family's safety. They had left Tyler County because their son Tom, their first child born in Texas, had almost drowned in a nearby slough. Hardin County, they found, despite its lush beauty, was equally filled with latent violence. Although orchids bloomed in the bogs, canebrake rattlers and water moccasins curled or slid silently across the familiar paths, and the heavy stillness that rose like a wall around them was often shattered by the shriek of a wildcat's fallen prey or the womanlike scream of a panther.

Martha Hooks was a practical as well as an imaginative woman—she allayed her own fears. She mixed backwoods vegetation and superstition—both of which she found in thriving abundance—into a veritable pharmacopoeia of home remedies. Her homemade camphor was a stock item on the family medicine shelf, and her concoction of corn whiskey and rock candy was a sure cure for the common cold, as well as for melancholia. She put a drop of kerosene on a lump of sugar for the croup, and she planted nut trees in her yard for lightning deflectors. A huge walnut tree scarred by lightning still stands on the grounds of the Hooks Cemetery, their earliest farm site, bearing witness to her ingenuity.

My favorite tale about her medicinal practices and powers concerns my father when he was a boy. He adored his grandparents and spent a lot of his childhood with them. It was on their farm, chopping wood with a Christmas hatchet, that he almost cut off his big toe. He loved to tell the story of that mishap; I must have heard it a hundred times. It seems his hatchet cut right through his copper-toed boots (the boots were also a Christmas present), and when his grandmother, to whom he ran for help, removed his stocking, she found that his toe was nearly severed from his foot. He was brave, and she was resourceful. She stuck his toe back on with resin from a pine tree that was growing in her back yard.

"And it isn't even stiff," Daddy always boasted, removing his shoe and sock and wiggling his toe to prove his point. My sister Pat insists that it was his second toe, not his big toe, that he almost cut off. Details in these family stories often become subjects of serious debate.

Besides dosing her family, Martha Hooks, called "Ma" by her children, seems to have clothed them as well. While others were spinning tales, she carded and spun the cotton from which she made almost everything they wore. From the fruit of her beloved walnut trees she made a dye that gave her otherwise conventional creations a little local color.

Both of my great-grandparents were firm believers in what you might call "reflective economy," insisting that, if you just put your mind to it, you could find a use for almost everything. Once when a batch of sweet potatoes in his storehouse began to sour, my great-grandfather hauled them all to Hooks Switch, where he knew a man who had a still, and had them made into two barrels of whiskey. Not as palatable as his accustomed brand, the liquor was, nevertheless, a potent brew that turned out to have curative powers. It so happened that, while he was running a fever, one of my great-uncles—Ben or Bud or George—broke into one of the barrels and sampled its contents. Whichever one it was, he not only got drunk, he also promptly broke out with the measles, which was evidently what was making him feverish in the first place. Consequently my great-grandmother decided that, while sweet potato whiskey certainly wasn't the most delectable of drinks, it was, as a matter of fact, a perfect prescription for making the measles run their course. And back in those days, medicine wasn't supposed to taste good.

The four Hooks brothers were, of course, followed to Texas by other members of their family, close kin and straggling connections. Some came by oxcart, some on foot. A rash but romantic bridegroom came on horseback, his bride of but a few days riding behind him in the same saddle. It is said that upon reaching an unfordable stream (possibly the same river in which Austin had drowned his ox), the determined youth stripped down to bare essentials and swam across, towing his young wife, who couldn't swim, by her long black hair. In one way or another they came, and by the end of 1870 the East Texas woods were full of Hookses.

Pap Hooks was a family man; he enjoyed being surrounded by his kin. He encouraged his brothers and sisters to follow him, and when his reluctant youngest sister lost her husband and was left with a houseful of children, Pap sent his son Day all the way back to Georgia to get her.

The perfect personification of the patriarch, he would go to almost any lengths to provide for his children. When his oldest daughter, Lucina, announced her engagement to young Dr. Silas Bryant Turner, Pap went all the way to Dallas in his oxcart to buy a barrel of white flour for the wedding cake and a pair of white satin slippers for Cine to be married in.

A fairly small man in stature, in the eyes of his family he stood eight feet tall in his stocking feet, the undisputed and unconventional lord of his own realm, master of all he surveyed—which, in the long run, was a large part of Hardin County. He rises like a jinn out of the rubbed-up reminiscence of Hooks family history, appearing in various guises, gratifying various desires.

According to everyone who knew him, he was a plain man. He contended that the airs people put on were like the emperor's new clothes, especially if someone else had sold them the bill of goods. He suited himself, and he judged a man, not by the cut of his coat, but by the figure he cut in his shirtsleeves.

His descendants have few affectations; their affinities with him spring up as naturally as mushrooms at the roots of an old oak. In their ranks, any rugged individualism, any disregard for dress or opinion that interferes with creature comfort is immediately attributed to "the Hooks blood in you"—scornfully sometimes by outsiders, always with the utmost satisfaction by fellow stockholders in the blood bank.

Eccentricity, that rare old bird, roosts comfortably in the Hooks family tree. Each generation seems to produce a few fledglings of the same unruffled feather.

"There was never anyone quite like Pap though," my father always insisted. He could have been more accurate than he imagined.

After all, no one gains immortality without being transformed.

—C. C. W.

4

Pap Hooks, Patriarch

I never saw Pap Hooks, of course, except in the old picture on the wall at the family homestead. I was told that he stood five feet eight inches tall and tended toward stockiness. The old portrait showed a man in formal dress with a wide brow, a straight nose, and grave, deep-set eyes that even in the photograph appeared to my bemused gaze to harbor a lurking twinkle. The rest of his features, however, remained hidden behind his most obvious and abundant physical characteristic, his hair. His leonine head was crowned with a thick, wiry, sandy-colored mane he trimmed himself, people said, whenever he felt that it needed it. His beard, which was merely a continuation of his cranial hair, was a mass of shaggy curls, which completely obscured the lower part of his face. His daughter Dode once remarked that she had seen her father clean-shaven only once in her life and that he hadn't looked a bit natural. A near neighbor who used to pass by his house every day remembered seeing him standing by the front gate, his foot propped on a stump, looking like a big hairy animal reading the *Galveston News*.

He was not only casual about his hair style, but, his portrait notwithstanding, he was habitually a little less than meticulous about his dress, a fact that is stressed, sometimes flaunted, in the famous shirttail stories told about him. A man who placed personal comfort at the top of his list of priorities, he often, according to the stories, conducted his home affairs dressed in his shirttail.

The precise meaning of this nebulous East Texas phrase is often unclear; however, its general gist is that the wearer of the "shirttail" wore no trousers, only a shirt of a somewhat debatable length. Small boys in the East Texas of that period were said to have worn shirttails, or simply elongated shirts. Perhaps Pap's shirttails, like those of the little boys, were elongated; then again, perhaps they weren't. At any rate, their length and what he wore under them (if anything) became, like the question of the Scotsman's kilts, subjects for heated family speculation throughout the years.

Convictions about these pertinent points always varied according to the disposition of the storyteller. Uncle Arden swore when he was relating the story to me that Pap's shirttail wasn't any too long. On the other hand, my mother, who is much more of a stickler, both for facts and for decorum, assured me that all shirts were made longer in the nineteenth century and that her grandfather's shirttails were certainly long enough to satisfy manly modesty, whatever he wore beneath them.

In my own favorite shirttail story, Pap was happily plowing his field one day, clad according to repute, when Lev Roberts, the temporarily estranged husband of his youngest daughter Dode, arrived at the Hooks house unexpectedly, probably hoping to mend the domestic quarrel. Ma Hooks, a diplomatic woman, promptly sent a pair of pants out to the field by one of her boys, hoping, I'm sure, that Pap would put them on before he came back to the house. Ma, Lev, and Dode were sitting sedately on the front porch making polite conversation when Pap, who loved to tease Ma, came around the corner, whistling. The pants were carefully folded over his arm; his famous shirttail was insouciantly waving in the East Texas breeze.

Pap may not have liked wearing conventional clothes, but he did wear them upon at least a few occasions, as evidenced not only by the portrait, but by the contents of an old trunk in the attic at the family homestead. In that trunk, among other conventional apparel, was an old formal dress suit that my mother said had once belonged to Pap's oldest son, William Columbus Hooks, who had met an untimely death during the War Between the States. Lum, a quiet, steady boy, had evidently been his parents' pride and joy. Extremely intelligent and well educated for his time and place, he had shown a great potential. For one thing, he had succeeded his father as commissioner of Hardin County before he was even old enough to vote. Meticulous like his mother, he was said to have been fond of fine clothes. It was his formal suit that was in the trunk, and the one in which Pap had been photographed, probably at Ma's insistence.

That picture, a bust view, became the standard family portrait of Pap, cherished and proudly displayed by his children and grandchildren alike. It was only recently, however, that my mother, rummaging through that old trunk in the homestead attic, found a print of the original uncropped photograph that revealed a hitherto unsuspected fact. Waist-length, it depicted the neatly and elegantly dressed family patriarch in his natural state of dishabille; the suit that fit him so perfectly around his shoulders actually gaped open at his waist, exposing not only a generous expanse of flesh, but his belly button as well.

Ironically enough, the formal portrait of Ma, the perfectionist, showed her with her glasses still resting carelessly on her forehead. She had probably been so upset about the way Pap's suit fit that she had forgotten to remove them. With his great love for teasing her, Pap certainly wouldn't have reminded her to take them off. His nonchalance about matters popularly considered weighty was notorious.

He had a healthy respect for the written word, however, an attitude which he bequeathed to many, if not most, of his progeny. His favorite book, the aforementioned *Travels of Baron Munchausen*, might just possibly have inspired some of the wide discrepancies in the Hooks family stories. Pap's favorite tale of Munchausen's was the one concerning "the wonderful effects of the frost upon his servant's French horn." In this tale, the servant's "tunes" were frozen up in his "horn" and came out only by thawing, so that "the honest fellow entertained Munchausen and company for some time with a variety of tunes," without once putting his mouth to the "horn." Pap had an earthy sense of humor, and this gusty tale tickled his funny bone.

A shrewd man, Pap seems to have made a fair amount of money over the years. It was said of him that he kept it all in the loft of his farmhouse; when he needed it, he would simply send one of his boys up after it. A contented farmer, he apparently accumulated even more land than cash; his gift to each of his children when they left home was a sizable farm. Bud, who was still living at home when his father died, was the only child not to receive such a gift. For this reason, when Ma Hooks died, Bud's siblings, or their heirs, presented Bud with that family homestead he had built for Ma on that knoll outside of Kountze. It was Pap's posthumous gift to his youngest child and inherent proof of Hooks family solidarity.

Not only respected but well loved within his small community, Pap had as his dominant character trait an easy, live-and-let-live geniality. According to all the stories, he was known to have lost his temper only twice. One instance involved a man who reneged on a horse trade; the other involved his son Day. The story goes that Day had come home roaring drunk—in broad open daylight—and that Pap, infuriated, had picked up a chair, preparing to properly chastise him. Day, however, in his astonishment at his father's rare display of anger, is said to have suddenly sobered up himself, relieving Pap of any responsibility and thereby restoring his usual good humor.

He seems to have been a particular favorite with children. Uncle Arden told me that a crowd of them habitually followed him around like mice after a shaggy Pied Piper. Instead of piping, he lured them after him with his teasing and the telling of tales. On one occasion, however, his love of teasing diminished his magical attraction in the eyes of a child, his prim and proper young granddaughter Josie Turner—a city child, who, it seemed, stood more than a little in awe of him. One day, while he was chopping wood in his yard, Josie and her parents came on a visit. Told to go say hello to her grandfather, Josie gathered up her skirts and her courage and gingerly started toward him. Pap, of course, had heard the exchange and knew she was coming. As she drew near him, he straightened up and, without turning around, roared in an awful voice, "I smell a little . . ." Josie, according to witnesses, fled the scene, horrified, not waiting to hear what it was she smelled like.

Pap was the object within his own family of an adoration that knew no bounds, a mild form of Shintoism that appeared to outsiders as mere clannishness but was to family members their most inviolable belief. In the hearts of his children, the image of their father appeared as an icon, tinted in the colors of East Texas earth but worshiped as a holy thing. Bud, who slept "on Pap's arm" until he was ten or eleven years old, in later years named his father as one of the five best men he had ever known. And on the back of that uncropped photograph of Pap, there is written in the hand of Orlou Ferguson, one of his older granddaughters: "William Hooks—one of the noblest men who ever lived." Each one of Pap's children named one of his, or her, sons "William." Day, his most prolific son, gave the honored name to two of his boys.

Pap had eight sons, some like him, some unlike him, each in his own way. Uncle Arden used to say that Pap and his son Buck would talk themselves out of a fight if they possibly could, that Bud and Ben would neither seek out a fight nor run from it, but that Day was like a ground rattler; he would sooner fight than not.

When the War Between the States began, Day was one of the first to join the Confederate army. Immediately thereafter Lum also joined, simply to keep Day out of trouble. As it happened, the patriotic attitude of all the Hooks boys reflected that of their father, and the sympathies of William Hooks were immutably with the South, although he owned no slaves. His father, George Hooks, had, upon moving from North Carolina to Georgia, either freed or sold—we've never been quite sure which—all the slaves ever owned by the Hooks family. Frankly, I've always thought that he freed them. I can't imagine bona fide Hookses ever owning another human being.

As fate would have it, Lum, his brother's keeper, contracted typhus in the Confederate headquarters at Galveston and was sent back home to die. His grave was the first in the Hooks Cemetery, and his father made his coffin with his own hands out of East Texas pine. Day, the daredevil, survived the war, after being captured by Yankees and losing half his toes from frostbite. Uncle Arden, who was a boy when Day died, told me that in his older years Day refused even to talk about the war—one Hooks, at least, in whom the urge to tell a tale had died a-borning. I understand that in his old age, he became one of the soberest men in the county.

Pap's third son, Buck, whose nickname demonstrates the correct East Texas pronunciation of "Alexander Buchanan," apparently inherited a large measure of his father's famous geniality. From his farm in the heart of the Big Thicket, where he raised canebrake cattle and fine horses, he extended a warm and impartial hospitality to friends and wayfarers alike. Reputedly, he was somewhat of a ladies' man. He once went to Houston to retrieve a favorite horse that his son, evidently another chip off the old block, had given to a young lady. The story goes that when Buck met the girl, he himself was so charmed with her that he not only decided to let her keep the horse the boy had given her, but he gallantly declared that, had he had another horse with him, he would have thrown that one in to boot.

Thomas Jackson Hooks, the first child born to Pap and Ma after their arrival in Southeast Texas, was also their first (and only) child to leave it. Suffering from a mild case of wanderlust, he eventually migrated to South Texas, where he settled his own small town, which he named Donna after one of his daughters.

George Washington Hooks, perhaps Pap's most intellectual and inventive son, had an analytical turn of mind which, in typical Hooks fashion, he used almost exclusively for his own personal pleasure. Like his brothers, he made most of his money in oil, but his principal reason for drilling the wells was simply to see for himself what was at the bottom of the hole. A frustrated scientist, he spent both his money and his time on one imaginative project after another.

The hobby for which I remember him best—for I actually knew him—was violin making. He, like his brother Ben, played good country fiddle. (Ben's rendition of "Cattle in the Canebrake," recorded with a cactus needle, is a collector's item.) George, however, following his analytical bent, was more interested in the actual structure of the instrument. During his lifetime, he made over forty fiddles, each of which he named—to mention a few, "Dewdrops," "Solace" (made the year his brother Bud died), and "Concerto."

The two Hooks brothers who inherited most of Pap's business acumen were Joseph Lamar, a good-looking man inexplicably called "Sam," and Jesse Benjamin, the illustrious Ben Hooks of my childhood memories. Sam and Ben were partners in several successful business ventures, including the sawmill at Hooks Switch. Sam, with only a touch of Tom's wanderlust, moved to Beaumont, but later, true to family tradition, returned to Hardin County to live out his life at Pine Knot, the farm given to him by his parents at the time of his marriage.

Ben, the shrewdest of Pap's sons, is said to have made three separate fortunes: one in whiskey, one in lumber, and one in oil. In 1904, he brought in the Saratoga oil field, almost singlehandedly. Using small hand pumps, which he called "strong-armed johnnies," and a hand-bolted derrick, he and a group of his friends and brothers brought in the well that was the very first in that great East Texas oil field. Ben personally oversaw the whole operation, staying at the well day and night. He said afterwards that he reckoned he was the first man to put a strainer on the bottom of an oil pipe to make it pour.

Like his father, Ben was a born leader, stepping confidently into his father's comfortable shoes. He spent his whole life in Kountze, leaving the indelible imprint of his personality on the town. It is said that he named most of its streets, submitting a list of suggestions inspired by the local flora and fauna. The list included such familiar names as Pine, Coon, Bear, Pisselm, and Polecat. The naming committee did not see fit to use them all.

Bud, Pap's baby son and my grandfather, was so undersized when he was young that Ma, acting upon an old East Texas superstition, had him chew tobacco as a cure for "the worms." Superstition or not, Bud grew up to be the biggest and best-looking of the Hooks men. Standing almost six feet barefooted (and he often went barefooted), he had the broad-shouldered, narrow-hipped build of a good athlete. Like Pap, he was notably casual about his personal appearance and thought nothing of going everywhere in his work clothes, which he did. He was particularly fond of good watches, fine animals, and expensive guns. It was said that if you saw a man in khakis wearing a gold watch, carrying a Winchester, and followed by at least two blooded hounds, that man was more than likely Bud Hooks.

In addition to their eight sons, Pap and Ma had four daughters, making an even dozen. All four were intensely supportive of their family, staying close to home and marrying "from around." They are all, with their husbands, buried in the Hooks Cemetery.

Amanda Luvenia, Callie's grandmother, was, according to one of her sisters, "the prettiest of the Hooks girls." Jane, who married Ed Chance, and whose full name, according to her tombstone, was Martha Ann Sarah Jane, probably had the most personality; there were lots of family gatherings at the Chance place. Dode, the youngest girl, christened Thedorah Eldoria, apparently had the sharpest sense of humor. Lucina Abigail, the oldest, whom Callie remembers as being a small, dainty, white-haired woman, seems to have had a strength of character that belied her fragile appearance. She reputedly had a lively interest in local politics, and although, being a nineteenth-century woman, she could play only a supporting role, she is said to have played it to the hilt. During the notorious Hooks-Lyons feud she dared any member of the Lyons family to walk in front of her house, threatening to charge them with trespassing if they did.

Pap Hooks was indeed the perfect personification of a patriarch. His family, like the stories told about them, spread so far throughout East Texas that in 1951 General Crude Oil Company, having oil interests in the Hardin County area, insisted that a complete affidavit on William Hooks and his kin be prepared, since any transaction with any of the people in those parts would probably involve his descendants to some degree. This affidavit was signed by the last of Pap's children to survive him, his tenth child, George Washington Hooks.

—E. W. R.

5

The Courthouse

There were never any cities in Hardin County. Most of its pioneers, for whatever reasons, seemed to prefer solitude to consolidation. Whether they sought to be fugitive from justice or far from the madding crowd, the early settlers of Southeast Texas found in the Piney Woods country a privacy they not only desired but stubbornly persisted to preserve. The Hookses, for all their initiative and ingenuity, were no exception to this rule. Collectively, they were prominent in the public eye, but, individually, they were very private persons, withdrawn into themselves, where they lived as comfortably and often as creatively as silkworms. When they first arrived and settled down in Hardin County, they were not fleeing from the law; they simply wanted to be one unto themselves. And, for a while there, they were.

After the county courthouse at Old Hardin burned down, the county seat was moved to Kountze, a small town built around a new courthouse and the various interests of the Hooks family. Except for the courthouse itself, an imposing structure of red bricks, all of the buildings in town—the stores, the churches, the houses, the one-story office buildings—were constructed of longleaf pine, cut at the sawmill owned by the Hookses. The names on the store fronts and the office shingles were the same names that were on the tombstones in the Hooks Cemetery.

There was a wild but widely circulated story that a Hooks—Gus, the eccentric son of Austin—had started the fire at Old Hardin. Gus was a capricious character whose strange antics were not all performed within the limits of the law—or even within the bounds of credulity. His most amazing performances involved his fleetness of foot. He seldom wore shoes and could run like a deer. At the courthouse fire, someone was sure he had seen Gus running away from the conflagration.

There are many stories about Gus's mercurial prowess. The best one concerns a footrace he ran and won against a man on a horse. It seems that his reputation for beating everyone who ran against him got around, and he was finally challenged by a man from Louisiana, a local champion, who rode over on his horse for the contest. After easily defeating his challenger, Gus, it is said, offered to run against his horse with him on it. Of course, he won that race too—by running backwards in front of the horse and successfully spooking both the rider and his steed.

"He would have won anyway," a member of his rooting section (and possibly of his family) said later. "That horse was handicapped to begin with—he was shod."

As for the story about the alleged arson, Gus was cleared of the charges. The evidence was purely circumstantial. Men on horseback raced miles through the Piney Woods to Gus's house on the banks of Village Creek, hoping to apprehend him, but when they arrived, their horses hot and frothing at their bits, Gus was sound asleep in his own bed. The implications of such a story were apparently ignored by the Hookses. But then they were never ones to put much credence in stories that they didn't tell themselves.

The new courthouse was monumental. I can still see it, standing stalwartly if gracelessly in the middle of the town, surrounded by pine trees and an aura of family history. We passed it every time we went to Kountze to visit relatives. Daddy always reminded us that as a boy he had helped in its construction, laying several rows of the red bricks with his own hands.

To me, it looked like something out of the *Arabian Nights*, although I am reasonably sure that it was fairly typical of country courthouses built at that time, especially in the South. It was a square building with a cupola on the top. (William Faulkner mentions courthouses with cupolas.) Encased in the cupola was the town clock, whose enormous hands struck off idle minutes with the measured efficiency of an executioner. If you stood close enough, you could hear them fall, like heads. In back of the building was the jail; it had a crenellated tower and looked like a medieval bastion, ostensibly designed for prisoners more romantic than the horse thieves and bootleggers it boarded.

Actually that courthouse was a family archive, emotionally as well as historically. It held collective memories as well as family records. Hookses had filed through its portals as familiarly as they had passed through their own front doors, leaving personal evidence behind them as plainly as they left their footprints in the red dust of the county roads. The walls they had helped raise echoed with their pleas as well as with their pronouncements. When the building was torn down—for it too has been superseded—Hookses came from all over Texas to buy the bricks, to build into a wall or a fireplace or just to use as bookends or doorstops. The courthouse had been a landmark in family as well as in county history.

Politics is in the Hooks blood, as indigenous to the stream as catfish are to Village Creek. In the early days of East Texas, the Hooks family not only created the political scene—even if it sometimes meant shifting the scenery—they also controlled the political climate. Occasionally it got a little hot.

According to the record, William Hooks always chose the sheriff of the county, being the only man around who had enough money to put up bond for him. It seems to have been an agreeable arrangement at the time. But times change, and as new families moved into the community and old families became more affluent, other stakes—and other voices—were raised. Political feuds began, usually over the question of the Hookses' inalienable right to run things. One such feud resulted in the fatal shooting of a Hooks in-law and an open gunfight in the streets of Woodville, Texas. Several seem to have resulted in broken romances. From the Hooks point of view, it was purely a case of other people's poaching on their prerogatives.

One of the families at political odds with ours—over prohibition, I believe—was the Dies family, a situation made somewhat awkward by the fact that my father's sister Elm was married to Tom Dies, who, at one time, was Hardin County attorney.

Aunt Elm is the central character in a stirring courtroom drama of the day. As I have said, politically the Hookses were like a stand of pines, moved only by the prevailing wind, and those who prevailed didn't like the Dieses' politics. The scene for the drama was set when Uncle Ben Hooks, duly elected spokesman for the Hooks clan, warned Tom Dies against using a certain piece of evidence in a case he had coming up in court. The action began when, on the appointed day, Uncle Ben, being a cautious man, went to court "to see for himself" that Tom didn't use it. One of Aunt Elm's younger brothers took her the news. She was in the middle of making mayhaw jelly.

"Uncle Ben has blood in his eye," the boy is said to have told her. The same blood stirred in the veins of my Aunt Elm.

She too went to court. She took her seat across the room from Uncle Ben and the clot of blood relations that had formed around him. When Tom Dies put his witness on the stand, the Hookses stood up—to be counted, I suppose. Across the aisle, Aunt Elm stood up also. People said that the courtroom was as still as the Thicket on a summer's day. For a second the Hooks aggregation didn't see Aunt Elm, but when they did see her, standing as firmly apart as a statute of the law, they all sat down—all, that is, except Uncle Ben. He continued to stand, and, across the silence of interrupted procedure, he alone met the unwavering stare of his older sister's daughter. Then, according to all accounts, he bowed to her and, taking up his hat, left the courtroom.

I never heard whether or not Tom Dies used the evidence. What Aunt Elm had to say was, "If anyone had hurt Tom that day, I was there to see for myself who did it."

"Of course, my jelly was ruined," she would usually add. "It sugared."

Daddy had two brothers who practiced law in Hardin County, my uncles Tom and Bryant Coe. Their first law office was in one of those small one-story buildings across the road from the old courthouse. They were both active in politics.

Uncle Bryant was Hardin County attorney for sixteen years. He could have been a writer. It was from him that I heard some of the better family stories. Sitting on the front doorsteps of his house in Kountze, listening to him recall or just plain reconstruct the past, I became irretrievably entangled in the family folklore that had already caught my fancy. With my ears perked up and my eyes bugging out of my head, I took in everything he had to say. The more my eyes bugged, the better his stories got.

One of the stories he told me involved the inimitable Gus Hooks and one of his sons, illustrating admirably that old adage about a wise parent knowing his own child. It seems the son had got himself into serious trouble, and, after a day in court, was sentenced to the state penitentiary. Uncle Bryant was district attorney at the time. After the trial, Gus approached him with admonition. "Bryant," he said, "you know there ain't no use sending that boy up there. He ain't gonna like it, and he ain't gonna stay."

Father knew best. The boy escaped so many times they quit coming after him, deciding, no doubt, to leave him where they knew they could always find him if they had to. That story was one of Uncle Bryant's favorites. Apparently it's a favorite among all the family storytellers; served up on frequent occasions, it has the unmistakable flavor of a family recipe.

A Beaumont man, one of his old friends, told me a story about Uncle Bryant. Only once in his colorful and comfortable career was he opposed for reelection; at that time a contender came up with the idea that the Coes and Hookşes had lived off the taxpayers long enough. Confronted with the problem, Uncle Bryant, according to his friend, confessed that he, for one, had never thought about it that way, but if that was what the majority wanted, he would be amenable to change, only not right then. He was unaccustomed to campaigning, he explained, but he promised, if the people would go to the polls and cast their votes for him as they had in the past, he would not seek political office the following term. He was reelected by an overwhelming majority. Two years later, according to his custom, he announced for county attorney.

"Mr. Coe," a voter is said to have reproached him, "two years ago you told us if you were reelected then, you wouldn't run again."

"Well, I'll be damned," Uncle Bryant reportedly exclaimed, "I lied to you, didn't I?"

Several hats were thrown into the air, his friend said, but not a one into the ring. The story is possibly apocryphal; it has a reverberating sound, and Uncle Bryant's friend was as good a yarnspinner as he was. It does, however, apply. Uncle Bryant held his office unchallenged until his death. He was succeeded by his son, H. A. Coe, and later, when H. A. became a judge, by a nephew, Stanley Coe, one of Uncle Tom's boys.

Uncle Tom, when he died, was chief justice of the court of civil appeals in Beaumont, to which he commuted, but prior to his appointment, he'd been district judge at Kountze for almost eighteen years. In the annals of Texas law he was a legend in, and of, his own time; during his term in Hardin County, his courtroom was a sort of school for young lawyers. Law firms throughout the state sent their bright young barristers "down to Kountze to try a case in Judge Coe's court." I have reliable reports that the experience was invaluable.

My husband told a story about a classmate of his, a classics scholar whose eloquent vocabulary flowed from his tongue as vintage wine from a full bottle. An eager and promising young partner in a large Houston law firm, he was sent, early in his career, to try a case before Uncle Tom. He did exceedingly well. After his closing speech, Uncle Tom praised him.

"That was a fine address, young man," he said. "Your points were well taken, your words beautifully chosen. Now do you mind if I tell the jury what you said?"

Country law, like country cooking, didn't always follow the book, and Uncle Tom had an educated palate. He knew when something had to be seasoned to taste.

There is one story about my uncles in the early days of their law practice that had its repercussions in a much later experience of my own. The story goes back to the time of their partnership in that one-story law office across from the courthouse. Young and impetuous, they were hotly embroiled in some political stew of the moment, a normal-enough pastime for Hooks progeny, when someone, to keep the pot boiling, pulled a gun on Uncle Tom. From what I heard, Uncle Bryant not only took the gun away from the man but, after he'd disarmed him, whipped him within an inch of his life. The story was reported by a young journalist on a Beaumont newspaper. Whether as a partisan of the other side or simply as a practitioner of purple prose, he described the defensive heroics of my impulsive uncle as "bloodthirsty." Uncle Bryant, in outraged indignation, made a rare trip to Beaumont to demand an apology. He got it.

Years later, I applied for a job on that same newspaper, taking carefully selected samples of my writing along with me. The young journalist who had so warmly covered the East Texas incident had by now become editor in chief. He interviewed me in his private office, reading with apparent interest my proffered pages of journalese. He didn't hire me, but he praised what he called my "sensitive style."

"You have a nice feeling for words," he said.

I thanked him.

"Which one of the Coes is your father?" he asked me.

"Burrell Coe," I told him.

"So Bryant Coe is your uncle," he concluded. "I know him well. He, too, has a strong feeling for words."

When the present courthouse in Kountze was completed, the Beaumont newspaper carried a picture of three Coes who were present for the opening session. District Judge H. A. Coe sat on the bench, and District Attorney Stanley Coe and practicing attorney Henry Allen Coe, Jr., appeared before him. When I saw the picture, an imaginary dialogue ran irresistibly through my head. It went something like this:

D.A. Stanley Coe: H. A., I'd like to make a motion.

Henry Allen Coe, Jr.: Daddy, I object.

Judge H. A. Coe: Objection overruled. Sit down, son, and quit interrupting. What's your motion, Stanley?

D.A. Stanley Coe: That we take a break.

Judge H. A. Coe: Court's adjourned.

That was, perhaps, the last closed alliance in our family.

There are no more Coes or Hookses playing principal parts in the political dramas of Hardin County—they have all died, retired, or moved away. I don't know who's keeping the store.

Early East Texas law may have been highhanded, but it was always forthright. Whether or not it's still carried on in the same tradition I can't say. Tradition, when it's as bold as brass, can become tarnished, especially when it's handled by those who are unfamiliar with the metal.

—C. C. W.

6

The Woodville Shooting Scrape

When the population of Hardin County exploded, politics, the lifeblood of many members of the Hooks clan, became bloody in earnest. The days when Pap Hooks had decreed the identity of Hardin County's sheriff had gone. The days that followed Pap's reign saw his boys on the scene, ready to defend the honor of their family, for other contenders had entered the lists, and the ensuing political feuds were, in reality, a manifestation of that primeval urge to protect those of one's own blood against all challengers, right or wrong. Sometimes assuming the proportions of ancient wars, these blood feuds implied both life's vital fluid and family loyalties, and the Hookses, with their veneration of family ties, were willing to spill the former to uphold the honor of the latter.

One of these political feuds provided what was perhaps the most spectacular incident in the lives of two of Pap's sons, Ben and Bud Hooks. I came by my knowledge of this affair, which became known as the Woodville Shooting Scrape, through two sources: one a yellowed newspaper clipping, a contemporary account of the event—the other my Uncle Arden, who, himself, had had it straight from the horse's mouth. As he related the story to me, I could perceive in the eye of this gentlest of Hookses a faint glint, a trace of the blood glimpsed in the eyes of the original protagonists and spilled on the dusty streets of Woodville a long time ago.

It seems that in a Hardin County sheriff's race just before the turn of the century, Dode Hooks's husband, Lev Roberts, defeated Bill Lyons, the incumbent sheriff. Several fights resulted from the outcome of this election, one of which took place on the streets of Kountze between Bill Lyons, backed by a score of his supporters, and Bud Hooks, backed only by his bird dog. Bud held his own, I am proud to report; an eyewitness said that every time he straightened out his arm, another Lyons man hit the dirt.

The main bout, however, took place in a local saloon between Lewis Ferguson, Dode's nephew-in-law, and Sam and Pleas Humble, who were partisans of Lyons. After the fight, as Ferguson was walking home along the railroad tracks, one—or both—of the Humble boys shot and killed him. He was found by the side of the tracks as the sun rose the next morning—according to the *Kountze Times*, "in the pale and cold embrace of death, shot down, like a brute, by the treacherous hand of an assassin."

As may be imagined, the murder was a nine days' wonder in Kountze, and the fact that Ferguson was a prosperous, well-loved merchant in town as well as a member by marriage of one of the oldest families in the county made the incident assume even larger proportions. The *Times* reported:

> Upon the discovery of [Ferguson's] body, the news was borne from lip to lip till the whole town seemed to veil its face with grief. . . . Few they are who did not love him with a brotherly love. . . . We who knew him best loved him best, but the many who frequent our town for business or recreation will feel that they have been robbed of a friend that time cannot replace. We can never forget his walk across our streets. We can never forget his unequalled magnanimity.
>
> No, indeed, time can never corrade [sic] the chain that binds us to him, nor can any change in abode or business ever efface the sorrow that weighs so heavily upon us. He was our friend; words can not tell our grief. I am overcome with sorrow. I cannot write.

The squib was signed, "Verily a Friend." He seems to have had many; besides which, there were all those Hooks in-laws.

On the day before the murder, Orlou Ferguson, Lewis's wife, had ridden the train to Beaumont, bent on a shopping trip. The night Lewis was shot, she inexplicably awakened from a deep sleep and glanced at the clock, noting the time. When the train bringing her back to Kountze pulled into the station, she apprehensively noticed a crowd of Hookses gathered on the platform. Their collective purpose, of course, was to break the tragic news of her husband's death before she learned it from anyone outside her family. She discovered in talking to them that the time she had noted on the clock corresponded exactly to the time of her husband's murder—a strange coincidence, or perhaps just another example of Hooks solidarity.

While the town was still in a state of shock, Sam and Pleas Humble, the accused murderers, disappeared. Their father, old Jim Humble, a good man, seemed to want to find them, but nevertheless, he failed to turn them up. My grandfather, Bud Hooks, one of Lev Roberts's deputies at the time, was standing at a window in the Hardin County courthouse when he saw Sam and Pleas go into the Thicket in the general direction of Cypress Creek. Keeping his distance and hoping to stay hidden, Bud followed them into the woods. When he heard a whistle, he figured they were meeting someone, and, alerted, he stealthily approached the scene. Even so, he surprised the gathering—or they surprised him—much more suddenly than he expected. Sam and Pleas were standing there, in a clearing, and so were old Jim and the youngest Humble boy, Billy. All of the men were armed. Billy had a shotgun in his hands, and he seemed, Bud said later, to be extremely nervous. Afraid of what Billy might do with the gun, Bud had immediately started talking. He had never waxed so eloquent in his life, he confessed. He had begun by saying, "Well, Jim, I see you've found them," and had continued in the same vein, trying hard to persuade them to give themselves up. Either Bud was very persuasive or the Humbles were dumbfounded by his sudden appearance, because they went quietly with him to the Hardin County jail.

When Sam and Pleas were brought to trial, feeling ran so high in Hardin County that the venue was changed to Tyler County. The case was tried there, and the jury acquitted Pleas Humble. Sam Humble was convicted of manslaughter but sentenced to only five years in prison. However, the prosecuting attorney, suspecting that the Humbles had a strong partisan on the jury, deliberately made a reversible error. In his jury argument, he pointed to Sam and said, "There he sits silent in the face of this damning testimony!" Sam, of course, was granted a new trial, just as the prosecutor had planned. An attorney's comment on the defendant's refusal to testify automatically calls for a new trial, and that prosecutor was determined to have another crack at Sam Humble.

It was to the second trial, on June 8, 1896, held in the Tyler County courthouse in Woodville, that people flocked, including men who avidly supported both sides of the affair. Bud and Ben went to Woodville as Ferguson supporters, of course. Other Ferguson partisans were Ped Ferguson, Lewis's brother, and Hardee Turner, the only brother of Lewis's widow. Both sides suspected that there would be shooting, so all of the men came armed. Ped Ferguson stationed his younger brother across the street from the courthouse, supplying him with several Winchesters and strict orders to pass them out if necessary. The trial went on until noon, when it was adjourned for dinner. Then everyone filed downstairs.

Ped Ferguson, hot-headed and hopping for revenge, spat inflammatory words on the way down at old Jim Humble. Jim retaliated. Ped, enraged, reached for his gun, but Hardee Turner, a cautious man, succeeded in staying his hand.

"For God's sake, man, let him alone," Ben Hooks warned Turner.

The warning came too late; Ped's advantage was lost. The Humble partisans had already drawn their guns. When the crowd broke onto the street, the shooting started. Bud and Ped Ferguson found themselves shooting at old Jim himself, who, unafraid, walked straight toward them, steadily firing his gun. Bud afterwards admitted that the barrel of Jim's gun looked all of six inches around. When it finally clicked on an empty chamber, Jim yelled at Bud, "Go ahead and shoot, goddam you, I'm out of ca'tridges."

"Oh, well, if you're out of ca'tridges," Bud replied, "I'll go shoot at somebody else."

The fracas developed into quite a scrape. A nonpartisan bystander caught one of the Humble boys shooting from behind a tree; he was so outraged at such behavior that he stuck a gun in Humble's ribs and made him move out into the open. Then Ben, a little behind Bud and Ped, noticed gunfire coming from the direction of the courthouse. Looking closer, he saw that it was coming from a side window. Incensed at such blatant cowardice, he entered the courthouse and discovered young Billy Humble firing at Bud and Ped from cover. Ben said later that as Billy turned and saw him, he looked almost ashamed, then made an awkward attempt to hide his gun. His action was not as quick as Ben's temper, however. In a split second, the infuriated Hooks had put his gun to Billy's stomach and fired.

Most of the reports have it that, although there were more than thirty shots fired altogether, everyone shot far too fast to do much damage, so there were not many serious injuries. Billy Humble's stomach wound was the most serious; people generally believed that he would die. Old Jim Humble had numerous flesh wounds; Pleas Humble suffered a slight wound in the leg; and Bud had bullet holes in his coat and his oversized Stetson hat.

After their ammunition was gone, Sam and Pleas Humble and the defeated sheriff, Bill Lyons, took to their heels—one of them was said to have vaulted a high board fence and left on a dead run—but old Jim, head of the clan, walked away. The Ferguson partisans went for their stashed Winchesters, but by that time the Tyler County sheriff and the judge before whom the case was being tried had come out of the courthouse to disarm everyone. Bud, armed, refused to give up his Winchester, afraid that the missing members of the Humble crowd might be hiding in buildings around the courthouse square, ready for sniping. Raising his arms, he held his gun above his head. The judge approached him and said in a stern voice, "Give me that gun, Mr. Hooks!" thereby gaining for himself a reputation for bravery. He did not gain Bud's gun, however.

Upon Bud's refusal to lower the gun, the sheriff and half a dozen other men grabbed it and tried to pull it down. The gun didn't budge. Bud would probably have held it up until someone thought of jerking his feet out from under him, but about that time, Lev Roberts, who had been up in the courtroom talking to a witness, came out and said to him, "It's all right, Bud. Give them the gun." Bud gave them the gun, but he, Ben, and Ped were put under arrest and their bond fixed at three hundred dollars each, which they readily paid. The charges against them were later dropped.

Billy Humble survived his wound; fortunately, Ben's bullet had hit a rib.

A family friend tells of a time, years later, when he, Bud and several other men were camping in the Piney Woods off the old Saratoga Road, waiting to go hunting the next morning. The men were just lying around camp when a stranger passed by. Bud, looking up, said nothing for a minute, then asked his friend, "Do you know who that was who just passed?"

"Sure do," the friend said.

"Who was it?" Bud asked him.

"Billy Humble," he answered.

"Sure was," Bud agreed.

That was the first time Bud had seen Billy since the shootout. The story goes that about thirty minutes later, they all saw Billy; he had turned around and was walking back toward their camp. It was at this point that someone anxiously exclaimed, "Good Lord! Here comes Billy Humble with a Winchester, and we don't even have a pine knot." Bud, always the peacemaker, got up and walked calmly out to the road.

"Howdy, Billy," he said casually.

"Howdy, Bud," Billy said.

That was all there was to it, Bud's friend reported. The two men shook hands and talked awhile, and just before Billy left,

Bud invited him to come back and go hunting with them that night. Billy said he might just do it, but, as it turned out, he was unable to make it.

The article in the *Kountze Times*, that yellowed newspaper clipping so carefully treasured by my family, was biased in favor of the Hooks faction, as I discovered the very first time I read it. The editor was probably a cousin. However, lest the reader suspect anything amiss, the last lines of the article put forth this disclaimer: "This is a correct statement of facts in the case and any contradictory statement is a base fabrication originating in the mind of some designing person who either desires to injure some one or to further his own selfish interest."

—E. W. R.

7

The Piney Woods

Geographically, the Piney Woods of East Texas extend from the Red River almost to the Gulf of Mexico. The heart of the woods, so far as I am concerned, lies somewhere close to Hardin County. The entire area, for me and for many others, I am sure, is spellbound, enchanted as it is by horned owls, flying squirrels, carnivorous plants, and imaginative storytellers. A large stretch of this heavily wooded land is all but impervious to the direct rays of the sun; it is, however, magically pervaded by a strongly slanted light cast on it by its denizens and devotees. These devoted denizens include, of course, any number of Hookses.

In the old days, I was told, the ivory-billed woodpecker, a bird almost as legendary as the roc, inhabited these woods, living in the giant pines that were later cut down by the early settlers and enterprising lumbermen. Too large to nest in any but the oldest and biggest trees, after those were destroyed, the beautiful bird, it was said, died out. Legitimately larger than a crow, when it was measured by the footrule of folklore, it acquired the size and symbolism of the American eagle.

Another fabulous creature of the Piney Woods, so faithfully evoked in those East Texas stories, was the black panther. Reputedly, it was as black as soot and screamed like a frightened woman—genetically unlike most other panthers, which were brown and went about quietly. Some folks refused to believe in it, but most East Texans did, and my credulity was devout. I remember one story, a cautionary tale, about a skeptical farmer who, upon hearing a shrill, womanlike scream in the night, rushed out with his shotgun to rescue a maiden in distress, only to see what looked like a large black cat dropping gracefully over the fence and disappearing into the woods. Unable to decide whether his eyes or his ears were deceiving him, he refused to shoot. The next morning, to his chagrin, he discovered that, from either an act of chivalry or a chauvinistic disregard for popular belief, he had lost a calf.

There were lots of tales about a place called Pigeon Roost Prairie and about how it came to be called by such an unusual name. A barren strip of land between Beaumont and Kountze, it had once been a forest, people said, boasting a full growth of majestic pines. Daddy's story was that one year a fabulous flock of pigeons had flown over, darkening the sky, and that, roosting in the pines, they had gradually broken off all the branches and eventually killed the trees, adding insult to injury by permanently ruining the soil with their copious droppings. According to some storytellers, Daddy explained, the droppings were often ten to twelve feet deep—and that's pretty deep, even for East Texas. His story, however, was apparently authenticated by no less a naturalist than John James Audubon, who is said to have a corresponding account of this phenomenon in his journals. Truth may or may not be stranger than fiction. It's hard to differentiate between them.

I instinctively enjoyed such tales, old and colorful yarns pulled out of the solid homespun of regional history, but the tales I enjoyed most were those about my own family and their natural affinity with this fabulous if not always fertile land.

My great-grandparents, pioneers who had prospered as well as multiplied, had given each of their children, when he or she married, an East Texas farm for a wedding present. My father was born on one of those farms, the first child of Amanda Luvenia Hooks and Henry Isaac Coe. The sound of the wind in the pine trees was his lullaby. Those oft-told tales, whether of sentiment or superstition, were his catechism.

When William Hooks, my great-grandfather, sent his son Day back to Georgia to get his widowed sister and her family, my Grandfather Coe, an orphan boy from Alabama, joined the wagon train on its return trip to Texas. Two years later he married my grandmother. Legend forms and clings like lichen on the Hooks name; we heard few stories about our Coe ancestors. My grandfather, it seems, talked very little about his family. He was born in Alabama, we were told, and, while he was still quite young, both his parents and several of his brothers and sisters died during a smallpox epidemic. Consequently, he was cheated out of his inheritance, evidently a considerable one, by either an older brother or an uncle. He was raised by several different families, none of them any kin. By his own account, he grew up like an unpruned shoot. He came from Alabama to Texas not to transplant his painfully torn roots but to graft his severed relations. The Hardin County Coes are a fruitful branch of the Hooks family tree.

Like Pap, Henry Coe was a farmer, a man of the soil; he was unlike him in every other respect, being neither gentle nor patient, imaginative nor indulgent. In the Hookses flows the milk of human kindness—albeit a very rich milk with the cream skimmed off the top for family consumption. In Henry Coe there was a vein of iron, its traces apparent in the only picture I've ever seen of him, in the glint of his eye and in the hard set of his prominent jaw. Perhaps because of his early experience, he was highly suspicious of human nature, although impeccably honest himself. It was said that he drove a fair bargain but always used his own nails. In the small community composed mostly of his wife's relatives, he was more respected than beloved.

My Grandmother Coe had a hard life; Henry Coe was not an easy man to live with—he had thunder in his soul. She herself, according to all the family stories, was as strong and steady as the morning light. She asked no more favors of fortune than the day asks concessions of the sun. She died in her early forties of typhoid fever, unremembered by even the oldest of her many grandchildren but enshrined in the memories of her eleven surviving children. I can still hear the tone of loving reverence in my father's voice and in those of his siblings when they began one of their stories with "our mother." It was her gentle hand that gave their childhood the lighter touch. It was her sure step on the path of least resistance that gave them their equilibrium. On her deathbed she made two requests, one of Aunt Elm and one of my father.

It seems she had promised her sons Tom and Ben a designated sum of money if they didn't smoke before they reached a certain age. She asked her oldest daughter Elm to see that they got their reward if they earned it, telling her not only where she'd find the money, but also where she'd likely find her brothers should they be tempted to surreptitiously break their bargain. She asked my father not to let her want for water after she became too weak to ask for it.

I have no idea at what ages Uncle Tom and Uncle Ben started smoking. I knew Aunt Elm quite well, and I am sure that, if they waited until the appointed time, they got their money. I am equally sure that, if they didn't, she spent the money for something else, probably books. She had by then started building her own library. My father stood at his mother's bedside and moistened her lips with a brush until she died.

Her picture shows a delicately boned woman with a mild look in her eyes; her eyes were as blue as cornflowers, my father said.

The children of Henry and Amanda Coe were an assorted dozen. The farmhouse they were raised in was a typical East Texas dogtrot house. A long, traditional hall ran all the way through it; the rooms were arranged on either side. Those halls, providing through ventilation as well as an unlimited vista, had their advantages and disadvantages. Aunt Elm told a story about my father that illustrated perfectly both points of view. According to her, she had just finished mopping the full length of their hall when one of Daddy's bird dogs walked across the floor with muddy feet. As she raised her mop to swing on the dog, she said, she was suddenly struck from behind with a half-eaten baked sweet potato. Sitting at the other end of the hall, unbeknownst to her, was my father, quietly chewing the last bite of something he'd been eating.

That story has always been one of my favorites, possibly because retained characteristics tend to give us a feeling of security, and, as long as he lived, my father owned bird dogs, loved sweet potatoes, and was a crack shot.

Aunt Lela Bruce, another one of his sisters, told a story with the same setting but a different tack. It concerned my father's sense of fastidious propriety, inherited, I suppose, from his grandmother. It seems that he was sitting comfortably on the front porch one day, having just removed his tie and the detachable collar men wore in those days, when, looking down the dog trot, he saw Mama, whom he was courting at the time, coming up the walk to see one of his sisters. Of course, he knew that she had seen him too, so he couldn't run, but not wanting her to catch him in his state of dishabille, he quickly improvised a collar out of his pocket handkerchief and held it around his neck until Mama was shown into the house.

"He was always a perfect gentleman," Aunt Lela said.

I'm sure he was, but then Aunt Lela thought all of the Hookses were nearly perfect. She refused to believe anything detrimental about any of them, regardless of her source of information. If one of them had a flagrant fault or sinned openly, he was simply taking after the other side of his family. For a while she had lived with her Hooks grandparents, keeping house for them in their declining years, and she worshiped them as household gods, giving them, if not actual obeisance, at least first place in her prayers.

Aunt Elm, of course, had no such familial illusions. She was a born bibliophile. She loved the English poets and believed, along with Keats, that truth was beauty, but she didn't always see a strong family resemblance to the Hookses on the face of it. Displaying a little of the pioneer spirit herself, she always thought there was a lot of room for improvement. An ardent student of Shakespeare, at one time she attempted to teach his plays in the public schools of Kountze. The Bard of Avon caught few fish on the banks of Village Creek, but Aunt Elm was dogged; she persisted in her project. One of her favorite quotations was from *Macbeth.*

"Lay on, Macduff, and damn'd be him that first cries, 'Hold, enough!'," she would cite, giving the quotation a strong East Texas inflection.

The women in my family, although they have blazed no trails of glory, have swept rather widely around their own doorsteps.

Daddy's stories always sounded as if he were talking to himself. They were mostly about his East Texas boyhood, spent mainly, it seemed to me, on Village Creek, swimming and fishing, or in the Big Thicket, hunting birds.

Village Creek is a fluctuating landmark in Hardin County, a movable feast, as it were. It meanders peacefully along its bed or wildly overflows its mudbanks, according to its mood. It is full of half-sunken logs, pools of quicksand and strange undercurrents that pull at you like frantic hands. It is also full of silvery fish and glistening sandbars. Its banks are shady and sheltered by a leafy overhang; the ground beneath the trees is soft. It was Daddy's favorite campsite when he was a boy. He caught his biggest fish in Village Creek, and once or twice he almost drowned in its treacherous waters. Lying on its banks, bedded down in oak leaves and pine needles, he watched the birds and listened to their sounds. He could imitate perfectly the calls of a screech owl or a bobwhite.

"Do you know what that old owl is saying?" he asked me once when we had both heard one in our back yard.

"No. What?" I asked, captivated by curiosity.

"'I cook for myself; who cooks for yoooo-all?'" he said, "that's what it's saying."

He was right. I've been listening carefully to owls ever since, and that is exactly what they're saying, a rather mundane remark, I must admit, to come from the mascot of Athena.

Daddy's other boyhood haunt, the Big Thicket, offered him more exciting adventures. At the time, its fabulous forest, besides burgeoning in folklore, was abounding in game: dove, quail, rabbits, wild turkeys, deer, and even bear. Daddy was strictly a bird hunter, but his two uncles, Ben and Bud Hooks, were avid bear hunters. A story goes that in one year alone the two of them killed sixteen bear in the Big Thicket, a fact especially remarkable since it had just been reported by some authority that there were only fifteen bear left in the whole area.

Uncle Ben and Uncle Bud were looming figures in Daddy's early background. His mother's two youngest brothers, they were both still living at home during those years when Daddy spent so much of his time with his grandparents. It was trailing after them that he first learned how to track game and how to handle dogs and a gun. Uncle Bud, I believe, gave him his first shotgun.

Daddy never killed a bear, but he did see a couple, one with its paw in a beehive. He loved to walk in the woods; his boyhood excursions into the Thicket had deepened his inherent appreciation of animal nature. He was a close and complacent observer. He enjoyed just sitting on a pine stump and watching a family of deer nibble at the dry grass, and he quietly reveled in the frenzied antics of his dogs when they treed a coon or an occasional wildcat. He said that one of the prettiest sights he had ever seen was a bird dog pointing a covey of quail, and at one time he kept a caged wildcat in his back yard, just because he liked to watch it move.

"And because Bud Hooks gave it to him," Mama used to add. The cat was apparently a prize specimen out of Uncle Bud's extraordinary menagerie.

As a boy, Daddy worked for his father on the family farm, where he decided that following a plow was not his natural pursuit. As a young man, he worked for his uncles, who, by then, one or another of them, owned everything in the county—tending bar in a saloon, minding the general store, and doing an assortment of jobs at the sawmill. It was the whine and whistle of the sawmill that he finally followed. He was twenty-five when he married my mother; she was eighteen. They lived under the aegis of the longleaf pine, moving from one small sawmill town to another. Joyce was born in Hooks Switch, Stewart in Kountze, and Herring in Loeb—all in Hardin County. The siren call of the mill eventually led them out of East Texas and into Louisiana, where I was born.

"Oh, you Louisiana gal, get your foot out of the mud and put it in the sand just as fast as you can," Stewart and Herring sang to me, and I cried—in abject humiliation at being the only member of my family to be born outside of Texas.

Mama had no patience with my vicarious provincialism; the chords of her nature were not attuned to the sound of the wind in the pine trees. She found the close environment of the woods claustrophobic. Somewhat of an introvert, she lived, during her years in East Texas, in an ivory tower of her own construction, a vantage point from which neither the forest nor the trees could obscure her own personal point of view. She followed the fashions of the times rather than of the place, ignoring local custom in favor of current trends. She dressed Joyce all in white to play in the red dirt of Hardin County and sent Stewart and Herring to country schools in sailor collars and Buster Brown haircuts.

"That's what all the little boys of that day were wearing," she insisted.

"Not in the Piney Woods, Mama," someone always objected.

Her invariable rejoinder was an ambiguous "Humph!"

The first sawmill town they lived in was Hooks Switch, a sprawling town built casually and consanguineously around the Hooks Brothers Lumber Company and a commissary, the exclusive dealer in all purchasable goods from beans to bedsheets. Mama ordered most of her children's clothes from Best and Company or Marshall Field's. The main street of the town, really only a dirt road, wound through the townsite like a dry creek bed, crossing cow pastures, dipping into wooded ravines and turning off into narrow sideroads that led to a scattering of houses. Laid out along the T&NO railroad track, that jugular vein of East Texas, the little settlement was still somewhat off the beaten path—no one there had ever thought of building a better mousetrap than you could buy at the commissary.

The house my family lived in was big and white and sat back off the road in a clump of pines. The long approach to it was lined on either side by a row of sycamore trees. The house had originally been built for one of the major stockholders in the lumber company—one of the Hooks brothers or Ben Herring, Mama's uncle—but he, whichever one it was, had preferred to live in Kountze and had offered the house to my parents. Mama loved those sycamore trees; their leafy symmetry seemed to provide her with a necessary sense of cultivated order. She would often stand in her doorway, she said, and gaze dreamily down the long walk, as through a telescope.

I did not inherit my pastoral proclivities from her. I did inherit her headstrong aspirations. The Coes and the Hookses were reasonable people; they believed you could see more stars walking from the back porch to the privy than you could from beating your head against a brick wall.

—C. C. W.

8

The Bear Hunt

Just after the turn of the century, with the aid of money they had made from the Saratoga oil field, Pap Hooks's two bear-hunting sons, Ben and Bud, built a hunting lodge in the middle of the Big Thicket. It was from this lodge that they began their avid pursuit of the Big Thicket black bear, a pursuit that became, for the two men, a passionate avocation. The bear hunts, an affirmation of their allegiance to the land, were for them an almost elemental rite, invariably taking place in the month of December, a traditional time for saturnalian festivities.

Intermingled with the mystique of the bear hunt was the vast, looming presence of the Big Thicket, that portion of the Piney Woods where timberland became jungle. Called by the Hasinai Indians the "Big Woods" and made legendary by European explorers hundreds of years ago, the Thicket lay, according to my Uncle Arden, in the shape of a huge sickle moon, curving from the small town of Segno at the northwest horn to the smaller town of Loeb at the southeast, thereby covering a large portion of Hardin County and of Southeast Texas. Only its denizens—animal and human—could navigate it. Newcomers to the area were consistently warned that, should they step even a few feet off a path, the Thicket would close around them and they might never find their way out of it again.

Having heard this admonition all my life, I decided one day to see for myself if it were true. While following Uncle Arden down a Thicket trail, I deliberately allowed him to disappear from sight, then, spotting my exact position, or thinking that I had, I stepped alone into the dense undergrowth. When I turned around, I found to my horror that the trail was gone. The trackless green wall around me gave no clue that there had ever been a trail, or, in fact, that there had ever been another human being within a hundred miles. Of course, Uncle Arden came back for me.

The Thicket was a place of many contrasts. Tangles of myrtle, yaupon, briars, and poison ivy grew out of an ancient leaf mold, creating an impasse for even the most seasoned traveler. Yet, at the top of an occasional knoll, great oaks and pines shaded out this underbrush, allowing easy passage for the uninitiated. These trees, their huge branches soaring upward, formed a vaulted ceiling over the forest floor. One could move freely through green glades of dogwood, sassafras, and magnolia, only to find that these pleasant glades suddenly gave way to steamy palmetto bogs, where water stood in stagnant pools and sundew grew in the moss, its sticky leaves open for unwary insects.

The Thicket was as deadly as it was magnificent. It was alive with animals: besides the small game, there were panthers, wolves, alligators, mink, and mosquitos, the infamous black bear, and razorback hogs that, with their sharp tusks, could slit a man's leg open in a second. There were lots of poisonous snakes; not only rattlers but cottonmouth moccasins, jewel-colored copperheads, and the deadliest snakes of all, the gentle innocuous-looking corals. As children, we were taught by a simple nursery rhyme how to distinguish between the deadly coral and the harmless king snake.

Red on black,
You're all right, Jack.

Red on yellow,
Kill a fellow.

By turns menace and solace, mortal enemy and primal womb, the Big Thicket cast its verdant spell over all who approached it. Members of the Hooks clan, especially Ben and Bud, easily succumbed to its sorcery. From their newly constructed lodge, the two brothers indefatigably hunted bear every winter, sometimes taking large parties of their friends and acquaintances with them.

The fame of their hunts spread so far that they actually attracted nationwide attention. Even Teddy Roosevelt, the old Rough Rider himself, once planned a hunt with the Hookses. Ben and Bud had it arranged so that Roosevelt could get off the train at Hooks Switch to avoid publicity; neither the President nor the Hooks brothers desired it. Unfortunately, affairs of state interfered, and Roosevelt was unable to make it.

One famous guest who did make it, however, was the legendary hunter and woodsman without peer Ben Lilly. Engaged at the time in hunting specimens for the Natural History Department of the Smithsonian Institution, Lilly came in 1905 to hunt with Ben and Bud and stayed, camping out around Bud's house, for almost three years. Uncle Arden remembered him as a large, ragged man with blue eyes, a black beard, and a perpetual smile. My grandmother remembered his meticulous politeness. She complained, however, that his Sunday clothes, which he donned only for dinner at her table, were just a little less ragged than his hunting clothes. He was a natural man. He never slept indoors; he simply curled up under a tree in the yard or in the woods and went to sleep. Arden said that you could set him down anywhere in the Thicket and he'd be able to find his way out, and that he could call up a deer simply by rubbing a pair of antlers together.

Lilly was present on the famous bear hunt of 1906, the most widely publicized, both in family stories and in national coverage, of all the hunts. Among the distinguished members of that particular hunting party was a feature writer for the *Topeka State Journal* named A. L. Kiene, who rode the Santa Fe from Kansas to Kountze for the occasion. His account of the event, entitled "Ten Days in the Big Thicket" and published in the Topeka paper, provides a fascinating blow-by-blow description of an East Texas bear hunt. When I read it, more than fifty years after it was written, it provided me with a rare glimpse of my family's private world as seen from an outsider's point of view. Of course, Kiene, uninitiated as he was, missed a few interesting details, but my myriad tale-spinning relatives were both able and willing to pick up any loose threads in his narrative.

According to their combined accounts, on that chilly December evening in 1906, the hunting party gathered, as was its wont, at Bud's house, the old Hooks homestead, on the very edge of the Thicket. There the hunters loaded their supplies, collected their dogs, mounted their saddle horses, and struck out for the bear camp, taking the old Saratoga Road. As they traveled, the Thicket closed over and around them, blotting out the last vestiges of the cold afternoon sunlight and plunging them into shadow. It was nightfall when they finally arrived at Hooks Lodge, a simple two-room pine cabin with the requisite East Texas front porch. Here, Ben Hooks and his brother Bud, "princes in their own realm," as Kiene called them, reigned supreme.

As the hunters unloaded their packs, Abe and Charley, the camp cooks, kindled a pine-knot fire, filling the wintry air with the sharp smell of fresh pine smoke. Gathering around a big pine trestle table set up in front of the porch, the exhausted guests eagerly awaited their first meal in the woods. When it came, the hearty supper consisted, as always, of squirrel stew, homemade bread, and baked sweet potatoes. After supper, the men squatted around the slowly dying fire, sipping coffee from tin cups and planning the next day's hunt. The following morning, up early in the cold December dawn, they saddled their horses and called up the dogs.

Ben and Bud together owned eight of the finest bear hounds in the county, an incomparable pack: Ramsey, Buck, Ring, Drag, Alec, Big Foot, Jack, and the legendary Dandy—the start dog, the most important hound in the pack. Dandy was a big redbone hound that was originally trained to run panther, but, reputedly, after running his first bear trail, had refused to run anything else but bear. His chief virtue was his sense of smell, and since he was far too valuable in this capacity to risk in a fight with the bears, the hunters would allow him to work up the trail, then pull him out when the trail got hot enough for the other dogs to find. Dandy became deaf in his old age and moved increasingly slower as the years went by, but he remained the best bear dog in the Thicket; no dog ever topped him.

Ben, master of the hunt and the dog handler, necked up all the dogs two by two—all, that is, except Dandy, who was allowed to run loose. Mounted, the hunters followed blazed trees into the heart of the "Hurricane," the most impenetrable part of the Thicket and a natural habitat for bear. The Hurricane was so called because a tornado had once destroyed all its big trees. Bear hunts always started in the Hurricane—and often ended there. Just off Lightning Trail, another landmark, the hunters, as was the custom, drew up their mounts and waited for the infallible Dandy to smell out a bear. Rummaging through the dead leaves, rustling and snuffling as he ranged in ever-widening circles, the elderly hound eventually moved off into the rank underbrush, and the men waited in expectant silence.

When the deep baying of the old dog came through the Thicket, signaling that he had at last struck a bear trail, Ben, the hunt master, sang out, "Here they come, boys," and straightaway freed the other dogs. Filling the air with a cacophony of barking, yelping, and baying, the pack headed straight for Dandy, soon far outdistancing him in their headlong pursuit of the prey.

With all the dogs hot on the bear's trail, Ben, relieved of that responsibility, took charge of the hunters, placing them at various vantage points. In accord with a kindly conspiracy hatched up the night before between himself and Lilly, Ben sent the tenderfoot Kiene to Gum Stick Pond, a small stagnant pool just a little way north of the Hurricane, the place where he figured Kiene would most likely encounter a bear. Ben and Lilly, then free to hunt, followed in the wake of the dogs.

By his own account, Kiene, the novice, waited at his station for about half an hour, then, either feeling forsaken or growing impatient, he set off in search of the action. On Lightning Trail, he again encountered Ben Lilly, who, still trying to put him in touch with the bear, told him to ride down another trail toward Black Creek. As Kiene rode down the narrow trail, his knees skinned by tree trunks, his face lashed by overhanging branches, he heard through the woods the raucous yelping of the bear pack. Dismounting and tying up his horse, the Kansan, perspiring in spite of the chill in the air, shouldered his Winchester and nervously began to work his way through the undergrowth, determined on a showdown with both dogs and bear.

He suddenly came upon them in a small clearing. The bear, at bay, his front feet on a fallen log, was snarling and snapping at the dogs, who were barking warily from a respectful distance. Automatically, Kiene aimed his rifle and fired. The forty-four-calibre rifle ball struck the bear squarely in the shoulder. It grunted, turned, and ran crashing through the brush, closely followed by the dogs, who, well trained, had at the sound of Kiene's gun sprung forward. Left behind by the fleeing bear and the pursuing dogs, Kiene struggled to follow them through the woods. Before he reached them, however, he was met head-on and knocked sprawling by a pack of frantically retreating hounds. Picking himself up, he pressed on, his rifle ready, the hounds now at his heels, only to discover a few yards ahead the inert form of the bear, which had apparently dropped dead just as it charged the dogs.

As the hounds, with revived courage, worried and bit at the carcass, Kiene shakily lifted his borrowed cow horn to his lips and inexpertly attempted to sound the three horn blasts that would summon his fellow hunters to his side. As he himself later put it, he blew until he thought he would burst, then fired his Winchester and hallooed until he was hoarse; still no one answered. He was finally found by Dandy, who was still trailing the dead bear, and eventually by the other hunters, who were trailing Dandy. The monstrous hound, still baying loudly, lumbered up to the bear on his heavy legs, sniffed, then settled himself proprietarily between the two front paws of the dead animal, triumphantly claiming his trophy.

When reproached for not heeding Kiene's summons, Ben Hooks admitted that he had heard the horn blasts but had ignored them. "I figured it was just some damn fool who was lost," he said, "and I aimed to let him stay lost until after the hunt was over."

Kiene wrote in his article that there was a note in Ben's voice indicating that the man Ben thought was lost was the man who had actually shot the bear.

The Hooks brothers and their friends congratulated Kiene on the kill, which, according to some family stories, they had engineered in the first place. A one-shot kill, particularly a shoulder shot, was somewhat of an accomplishment even for a seasoned hunter; for a novice, it was a miracle. And few Hookses believed in miracles, unless they themselves played an active part in their performance.

They tied the bear across Kiene's horse and made their way, in the lengthening shadows, back to Hooks Lodge, where they threw the bear upon the trestle table and skinned and cleaned it amidst much laughing, joking, and telling of tales. The skin, with the head still attached, was stretched upon a square sapling frame and suitably prepared for the floor in front of someone's fireplace. Squirrel stew was not in evidence that night; instead, the hunters feasted upon succulent bear steaks, later playing fan-tan around the table by the flickering light of the camp fire.

Bud, the wit of the camp, invariably entertained his fellow hunters with tales of former bear hunts. Perhaps that night he told them of one of his own moments of truth, a story that was told to me sixty years later by one of Bud's and Ben's younger friends, himself an old man by the time I heard the tale from him. It seems that on one of the hunts, Bud, being the first man to reach a treed bear, took the shot that was his prerogative before any of the other hunters arrived on the scene. The shot dislodged the bear, apparently a big one, from its perch, and the huge animal came crashing to the ground just behind Bud, where it crouched on all fours, momentarily stunned by its fall. Bud, turning swiftly, pointed his rifle at the animal's head, aiming to kill. The enraged bear, however, suddenly regaining its senses, reared upon its hind legs and turned on Bud, catching his gun in its teeth. Bud pulled hard on the gun, but the bear pulled harder. Things looked serious until someone else arrived on the scene, instantly assessed the seriousness of the situation, and quickly shot the bear.

"For a few minutes there, I was afraid I was going to be shot by an animal," Bud said later, "and with my own gun, at that."

Bud's rifle, when examined, had teeth marks on it eight inches long. Its usefulness was unimpaired, however, and Bud used it for many years before he gave it to his nephew, Bryant Coe, Callie's storytelling uncle.

As the years went by and Ben and Bud grew old in Kountze, the black bear all but disappeared from the Big Thicket, helped on its way, no doubt, by the hunting activities of the Hooks brothers. The bear hunts of that magic decade faded gradually into the realm of legend, growing in story as they receded in time. The Thicket, too, dwindled in physical size as more and more settlers moved into the area; its boundaries, always a matter for speculation, were gradually hacked away until it scarcely bore a resemblance to its original state.

The spell of the Thicket remained, however, and continued to exercise its enchantment upon its inhabitants; few members of the Hooks family have ever completely lost their yearning for the woods.

—E. W. R.

9

Shifting Patterns

Thomas Wolfe was wrong—you can go home again, just not by the same way you left. You almost always do return—but usually by some circuitous route. Familiar paths become overgrown, and a one-time wilderness, properly weeded, becomes a wayside park. Landmarks disappear into landscape. Continuity runs an obstacle course.

We all follow our noses, features inherited from our forefathers, more often than we think. My own nose, sniffing out the past, recently led me back to Hardin County, that scene dominated, if not actually created, by my ancestors. I was accompanied on the trip by my cousin Ellen. Ours was a sentimental journey, a pilgrimage with a picnic lunch. Our main purpose was to reexplore the ground we had just covered in the family chronicles we were writing, or, in plainer language, to cover our tracks.

It was April, and the evidence of spring was everywhere. The woods, as we drove through them, glistened in a wide variety of forest greens, and the dogwood, the haw, and the honeysuckle were all in full bloom, creating a strong undertow of light in the heavy brush that grew along the highway. Loose fragments of an early morning fog were caught in the trees, looking like tattered garments hung out to dry, as though Mother Nature, a wanton, had washed her dirty linen in public. An exhausted wind, up all night, was barely blowing, and a bright blue sky was stretched like a tent over an already active countryside.

"It's beautiful," Ellen said emphatically.

I agreed.

"'Breathes there the man with soul so dead,'" I began the familiar lines of Scott. For while the red earth of Hardin County was not exactly our "native land" (I was born in Louisiana, Ellen in Beaumont), it was, after all, the land that William and Martha Hooks, our great-grandparents, had settled—for a while anyway.

We were searching for the physical evidence of our common past, the secret door to which we had opened, like Ali Baba's cave, with the magic of words we had simply overheard. Having squandered the stored-up treasure, we were looking for the mother lode.

We stopped first in that part of the county that had formerly been Hooks Switch, the small sawmill town owned and operated by members of the Hooks family. It was now a gun club and shooting range, surrounded by a prospering tree farm that belonged to the local paper mill. I looked around for the place where my parents had lived.

Ellen parked the car along the highway. "According to what you've said, it must have been right about here," she suggested.

I got out of the car. Crossing a ditch and crawling under a barbed-wire fence, I confronted a large, straggling row of giant sycamore trees. These stragglers, I concluded, were undoubtedly the only survivors of that arboreal avenue that had once led to my parents' house.

"There used to be a double row," I explained to Ellen, wondering if the other trees had died or been cut down.

Standing there, with the weeds tickling my ankles and making me want to scratch, as they had years ago in the Hooks Cemetery, I attempted to reconstruct the past in my mind's eye. I had never lived in Hooks Switch; my family had lived there long before I was born, and the memory that's in the blood does not always have total recall. My projections, instead of being Proustian, were as fragmentary as phrases.

I could see my mother, a young woman, strolling down the tree-lined walk to the dirt road, holding Joyce, an apparition all in white, by the hand, and I could see Joyce, a beautiful child, stooping to wipe the dust off Mama's shoes, using her clean handkerchief—just as Mama had told me she had done. I could hear the crickets and the tree frogs and the five o'clock whistle of the sawmill as it split a quiet afternoon into shreds of sound and sent my father homeward. But, somehow, no matter how hard I tried, I couldn't see the house itself, although I had heard it described a hundred times, or hear the noises that had given it life. A modern brick bungalow now stood on the spot where I supposed the old house had stood; its presence seemed to be blocking my point of view. The past is more easily discovered in ruins than in renovations.

"The sawmill was somewhere over there," I said, waving my arm as though it were a slightly defective wand, "and the commissary was across the road."

Oddly enough, I could almost see the commissary, a wooden structure as red as a country barn, its wide front porch extended like an oversized welcome mat. I remembered a story someone had told me about the commissary and its benevolent monopoly. Once, it seemed, despite the regularity of the old East Texas ritual of hog killing, the store had run out of meat for a rather extensive time, and my Uncle Bryant Coe, self-styled poet laureate of Hardin County, had raised his voice in song on the subject.

> Oh, my Lord, wouldn't it be nice
> To have some bacon to go with this rice,

he had sung. Surely, it was the first protest song to be heard in Southeast Texas. It was also a forerunner of my own first poem. At a very tender age, motivated by much the same sentiment, I had come out at the dinner table with:

> Deedle-deedle damn,
> Pass me the ham!

Believe me, blood will eventually tell, even if it doesn't always speak in rhymed couplets or, necessarily, when it's prompted from the wings.

We got back in the car, and Ellen drove down to what I was reasonably sure had been the old millpond. There were ducks swimming on its muddied surface. The gun-club members probably used them for their pigeon shoots, I decided. Getting out once more, I tossed a pebble I'd picked up into the dirtied water—whether in deference or defiance I still don't know.

On the way to Kountze, we passed through Pigeon Roost Prairie. A fresh but sparse growth of pines had sprung up haphazardly in the open fields, looking, with upright needles, like ill-arranged candelabra.

"They're growing back," Ellen observed.

I nodded. "Someone must have rehabilitated the soil," I said. "Before long there will be no prairie to prompt that old tale about the pigeons."

My childhood rose like a lump in my throat. There is nothing more tenacious than sentiment, and, like a bulldog, it always seems to get you by the throat.

Reaching Kountze, Ellen pulled up in front of the new courthouse, a boxlike building that held no memories for either of us. As functional as a balanced equation, it appeared to have no unknown quantities, no deviations of design. It provided no room for the romantic wanderings of childish imaginations.

"Wonder what happened to the big clock on the old courthouse?" Ellen asked.

"I don't know," I said.

"Do you suppose it still works?" she asked—anxiously, as though it had been keeping immortal time.

"I'm sure it does," I said, convinced.

We both took heart.

"Shall we go on to the library?" Ellen proposed.

"Of course," I agreed.

We had to ask the way, so we stopped at a filling station. The directions we got were explicit, but, after following the short, winding roads, we felt, when we finally arrived, as if we had accidentally stumbled upon the place. It was a small prefab building with a painted sign that said "Kountze Public Library." We had heard that it housed a plaque or bas-relief of Gus Hooks, celebrating his triumphant footrace with a horse.

Gus, that creek-bottom centaur, the most fabulous character in our family folklore, was now in the public domain. His most exciting exploit had been used by Temple-Eastex in a magazine ad, promoting the preservation of trees and tradition in Big Thicket country. Gus had become a legitimate folk figure, like Tolkien's Tom Bombadil and Pan. The plaque, which we found in the library, depicted a barefoot man outrunning a man on horseback.

"He was one of our local heroes," the young librarian explained eagerly.

We graciously acknowledged the fact, thinking of the various versions of that now famous footrace that we had both heard and, later, told.

Gus's publicity seemed to diminish him, somehow, the way a captured lion, caged and exhibited in a zoo, is diminished. He had moved freely and facetiously through our family stories; no one had ever tried to pin him down.

Unconventional to the point of being perverse, Gus had drunk soft drinks out of a whiskey bottle, whiskey, which it was rumored he made himself, out of a pop bottle—just to put people off, he'd claimed. He had been a talented bee man. It was said that he could "lead a swarm of bees ten miles through the Piney Woods, herding them like a sheep dog." He would lure the bees, folks said, by singing to them, a song he had learned from the bees themselves, just by listening to their humming. You might say that he had spoken their language. Probably because of this proficiency, it was believed by some that he'd kept his money, mostly gold, in his beehives.

He was an erratic character. His feats and foibles should never have become standard text. The Hookses, a sedentary family, never expected to have to rise to their tall tales.

William Humphrey, a Texas writer, says in his novel *The*

Ordways that "the Southerner will boast of ancestors whose memory another man would hide at the back of the highest shelf in his family skeleton closet."

True enough, but the stories told by the Hookses are more than just the funny bones of family skeletons. They are links in a carefully forged chain of family solidarity. It has often been said that no chain is any stronger than its weakest link. In the long, interwinding chain of Hookses, they themselves have soldered their weakest links with their own warm brand of humor. The chain has held together, strongly, but always with plenty of slack. "Give a relative an inch and he'll take a mile, a darn good distance to keep between you," is an old family adage closely observed by most members of the Hooks clan—at least as long as none of them are in trouble, that is.

Before leaving Kountze, we drove by Uncle Ben's house. No one lived there; the house and yard had been taken over by nature, that assiduous trespasser. The trees and bushes had gone wild, and the prying tendrils of a stray woods vine had pushed through the crumbling window sills and crept intrusively over the threshold of the front door. The whole place had been vandalized by time. Sadly we turned to go, casting last-minute looks, like hastily flung fishing nets, around us. I don't know what images Ellen came up with; my mind's eye caught Uncle Ben sitting on the front porch with his fiddle tucked under his chin, his right foot, encased in a high-quarter shoe, beating time to his music, probably his own personal rendition of "Cattle in the Canebrake." That seemed appropriate for a recessional.

We headed back to Beaumont.

"Let's stop by the Hooks Cemetery," Ellen said. "I haven't been there since Uncle Arden's funeral." Neither had I.

The road, once rough and meandering, had been straightened out and graded—a pastoral poem translated into academic prose. I missed the peregrinations and potholes. In no time we arrived at the cemetery gate, and Ellen parked the car in the clearing.

"Good Lord, they've taken out the old weeping water

pump, the perennial mourner," I exclaimed. "I'll never again feel properly received."

A spectral haze floated in the air; the cloying smell of cape jasmine assailed our senses. We stood there together, thoughtfully regarding the irregular rows of tombstones that appeared before us, a squatty skyline of the common past that we'd been seeking. The cemetery had grown, extending in all directions. The central part that had been set aside for family burial was full; there were Hooks graves outside the old iron fence that had once been the line of demarcation. My first cousin, Uncle Bryant's daughter, was buried outside the fence, I remembered. Some intruder without a drop of Hooks blood in his veins had inadvertently been buried inside the fence, in the space that had been reserved for her. She had been righteously indignant when she discovered it, her daughter had told me.

"Come the resurrection, I'll get the son of a gun," she had promised. I sincerely hoped she would.

Automatically, I walked over to the double headstone of my grandparents; it had once seemed to me to be as large as the Lincoln Memorial. It was just an average-size stone. I looked around for the grave of my sister Bernice, who had died in infancy and was the only member of my immediate family who was buried in the Hooks Cemetery. Mama had never completely overcome her objection to the woods. "I spent most of my life in those Piney Woods," she had said, "and I surely don't intend to spend eternity there." So Daddy had bought a lot in the Magnolia Cemetery in Beaumont. They are both buried there, as are Joyce and Stewart and "Bubby," Pat's son. Bernice had been buried too long for her body to be moved, we were told. I stooped and pulled up a weed that was growing on her grave.

"Here's Susie Roberts's headstone," Ellen called. "Did you know that she was only fifteen when she killed herself?"

Susie, our great-aunt Dode's only daughter, had been the romantically tragic victim of one of the Hooks family feuds. She had been caught by her brothers "keeping company" with the wild and handsome son of an opposing house, and when they had teasingly threatened to tell their father, who was away on a business trip at the time, Susie had taken poison and her life. The ill-fated rendezvous at the edge of the woods had been innocent enough; the Roberts boys, hunting squirrel or rabbits, had simply seen their sister sitting with her back against a tree with the young man's head in her lap. They had only meant to tease her, she to frighten them; but no antidote that she took (and they poured them down her) counteracted the carbolic acid she had swallowed. She died before her father got back from Beaumont. Her young man left Kountze and later became a doctor. The family feud was eventually resolved. She, of course, was immortalized in family stories, the hapless heroine of a rural idyll that, in our ears, had the resonance of a "Daphnis and Chloe" or a "Romeo and Juliet."

"Blood gets a little too thick sometimes, doesn't it," Ellen said philosophically.

We paused for a moment, almost reverently, in front of the tombstone of our great-grandparents. It was covered, as though draped, with the black fungus I remembered from childhood, and a moss-green patina that looked like official braid lined its numerous cracks. The inscription was almost obscured.

"'William Hooks, born 1818, died 1894; Martha Hooks . . . ,'" Ellen read with effort. Her voice seemed to trail off into the trees, like smoke from a dying fire.

We both gazed quietly around us, breathing deeply, as if the information we sought was not cut into the stones, after all, but wafted on the sweet-smelling air. It was cool, unusually so for the woods, we thought. The limbs of the trees quivered, stirred by the breeze; the birds sang unconcernedly. We walked around the cemetery yard, careful not to step on any of the graves, as we had both been cautioned against doing when we were children. Leaving, we once more looked back over our shoulders, still hoping, I suppose, to surprise some affirming spirit.

"They've ruined this road," I said, as we drove off, "absolutely ruined it. It used to be like a tunnel into the woods; now it's a throughway."

Nothing was like it was supposed to be, I thought, deeply despondent, not the way I'd heard it was or even the way I remembered it. No matter how colorful the Hooks stories had been, they had faded—maybe from overexposure, I admitted to myself. No one was interested in hearing them anymore. Ellen and I might just as well curtail our current chronicles. The ghosts had been laid.

A few months later I was in New York City, sitting with my two children in a restaurant, waiting to be served. While we waited, we fell into conversation with four attractive young men, obviously native New Yorkers, who were sitting at the next table. "Where are you from?" one of them eventually asked us.

When we said Texas, he smiled broadly and said that he was also a Texan, by birth.

"From what city?" I asked him.

"No city," he said, "just a small town in South Texas. I'm sure you've never heard of it."

I suggested that I might have. "What's the name of it?" I persisted.

"Donna," he said.

It was my turn to smile. "Donna, Texas, was named for a relative of mine, by her father, who settled it," I said, rather smugly, I'm afraid.

"Donna Hooks?" he asked.

"Yes," I said. "You've heard of her?"

"She was also a relative of mine," he announced. "My family were originally from Southeast Texas, from Hardin County. My great-grandfather was murdered in a town called Kountze by the Humble brothers."

I couldn't believe my ears.

"He was waylaid in the middle of the night," he went on to explain, "by a couple of assassins. His body wasn't found until the next morning. People say his bird dog sat by the body all night long—wouldn't let anyone get near it until the men who found him that morning woke up a near relative, a cousin the dog recognized."

My smile expanded, no longer smug but completely empathetic.

"Your great-great-grandmother and my grandmother were sisters," I told the young man. "We're kissing cousins."

"Well, if that doesn't beat anything I ever heard," one of his friends exclaimed.

I was sure that it did. It was a good story, one of the best—I could hardly wait to get back home to tell it. And it would be retold, I suddenly realized, by voices yet to be raised, perhaps by my own son, who wanted to be a poet. I could see that he was impressed. The Hookses had not lost their chronic charisma, after all. They were still being celebrated. The new generation of family troubadours, although they sang in a different key, were coming back around full circle to serenade the past. Family virtues would be extolled, and the sins of the fathers would be accorded the reception due visiting relatives. The Hooks Cemetery would continue to give up its ghosts.

This much I should have learned by ear—ancestors never die; they simply fade into the realm of the imagination, reappearing in the recollections of their descendants in renewed and vivid color, color often more vivid, in fact, than that claimed in the full flush of real life.

"You know," my son said, as we left the restaurant, "I never really thought all those old family stories were true."

"They are," I assured him, a little indignant at his lack of faith.

Truth, after all, is the patina that forms in time on fact.

—C. C. W.

Epilogue

William Hooks died at his home in Kountze on January 13, 1894, at the age of seventy-six. He was survived by his wife, eleven children, fifty-seven grandchildren, and fifteen great-grandchildren, most of whom were living in Hardin County at the time of his death. He was buried in the family cemetery near the grave of his oldest son, William Columbus Hooks, his only child to predecease him. From the time of Lum's death, it had been Pap's custom to make the coffins for all those relatives buried in the Hooks Cemetery; when he himself died, his two youngest sons, Ben and Bud, built his coffin.

That winter, Pap had suffered a severe case of the flu. The day of his death, he had prematurely risen from his sickbed to partake of his favorite meal—fatback and baked sweet potatoes. As he returned to bed, his staunch heart suddenly failed him. He died instantly. A Hardin County physician pronounced the cause of death to be "rheumatism of the chest." His obituary, which appeared in the *Kountze Times*, read, in part: "He outlasted his allotted time, but will be missed and sincerely mourned by those who knew him."

On that April morning when Callie and I revisited the Hooks Cemetery, I was shocked to realize that, according to the barely legible inscription on his mossy tombstone, our revered family progenitor, that baron of the backwoods, had actually been dead for almost a hundred years. It seemed to me that time, in its passing, had lost all chronological proportion.

Minutes later, I had another shock that confirmed this fantasy. A strange headstone, conspicuously new among its weathered neighbors, abruptly obtruded itself on my line of vision. The large letters carved on its shiny surface spelled inexorably: ARDEN HOOKS.

Although I had certainly been at Arden's funeral, I had not been in the Hooks Cemetery since his headstone had been erected; intent upon my childhood's hoarded image of this hallowed place, an image in which he, a living man, had often figured as one of my guides, I had for the moment forgotten his death. Faced with such indisputable evidence, I had to acknowledge that the Hooks family's principal raconteur was now interred among his belauded ancestors. His storytelling voice had been stilled. The stories had stopped.

I have since found, however, that, as Callie says, echoes from the past do reverberate and threads of family stories are not so irrevocably cut—at least, not if they are Hooks family stories. As a matter of fact, it is these unbroken threads that comprise our common family heritage—Callie's and mine. As strong and as durable as Ma's homespun cotton, they also continue to run through the personalities of our contemporary kin.

All the egocentricities of Pap Hooks that have so entertained his progeny continue to possess them. Callie's remark that her brother Herring didn't even bother to march to a different drummer generally applies. Pap's celebrated independence is present in nearly every one of his descendants, sometimes to a small, sometimes to an astonishing degree. This quality, which some people charitably call charm and others call just plain orneriness, is an innate autonomy, a reclusive streak that ultimately transcends all conventional sociability. Whatever the Hookses pursue, be it bears or bees, farming or fiddling, frenetic activity, or just plain cultivated idleness, most of them feel strongly that they must be left free to pursue it.

Pap's creativity and inventiveness of mind are manifest in

the sculptures and mathematical theories of his great-grandson Herring Coe, and those famous shirttail stories, so often repeated, have their modern reprise. Arden, with a total disregard for conventional attire, was, at his own request, buried in his habitual garb of khaki shirt and faded blue jeans, and Bryant Coe once declined an invitation to a family dinner party in Beaumont by explaining to the hostess that he couldn't come because he couldn't find his other sock. The hostess, being Sam Hooks's daughter, understood perfectly.

Pap's great passion for the land has also been handed down, even unto the third generation. A granddaughter of his beloved daughter Jane is said to have missed a Beaumont Country Club dance because she spent the money she had set aside for a new ball dress to buy two loads of fertilizer for her flower beds. That same granddaughter is now happily residing on the old Chance place—in Hardin County.

Family sentiment still runs in the same rich veins. One of my mother's most cherished possessions is a straight-backed, hide-bottom chair that is the mate (or at least a sibling) of that rocking chair that served the young Hooks mothers so well on their wagon trek from Georgia.

Family pride, that precious commodity, still comes high. Thomas Hooks, Uncle Buck's great-grandson, and Henry Allen Hooks II, Arden's only child, are, among others, indefatigable collectors of Hooks memorabilia; from Allen one day will come a definitive history of the Hooks family.

As for Arden's claim that he could recognize a Hooks anywhere—because either "she laughs like Aunt Dode," or "he walks just like Uncle Day"—most Hookses might not be able to spot a relative at first sight, but, once the relationship is established, they can easily recognize the family attributes. Once Callie's brother Stewart, an avid golfer, was just teeing off on his favorite course when a man in khakis with a shock of white hair asked to come through. Stewart apparently minded his manners, but muttered to his partner, "The old codger probably hits the ball with a hoe."

Before he shot, the man looked sharply at Stewart. "Hey, son, aren't you Burrell Coe's boy?" he asked.

"Yes, sir," Stewart answered, somewhat flustered.

"Thought so. I'm your Uncle Bud," the man confided, and, with one stroke, put his ball in perfect position on the green.

After a moment of stunned silence, Stewart turned to his companions. "Damn! Did you see that shot?" he exclaimed proudly—and proprietarily. "That's my great-uncle!"

As J. R. R. Tolkien, a favorite writer of a number of Hookses, once wrote, "The Road goes ever on and on, / Down from the door where it began. . . ." That magic door, for Callie and me and for all our kin, unmistakably lies at the site of that old grave in the Hooks Family Cemetery, where Pap is buried in the red earth near his first farm in the middle of the East Texas Piney Woods.

REQUIESCAT IN PACE.

—E. W. R.